GUIDE TO

INTERNAL CONTROLS

Under Section 404
of the Sarbanes-Oxley Act

James Hamilton, J.D., LL.M
N. Peter Rasmussen, J.D.

CCH INCORPORATED
Chicago

books\bu\simplecovers\filename.p65

Related CCH Titles

Sarbanes-Oxley Manual: A Handbook for the Act and SEC Rules

PCAOB Reporter

U.S. Master™ Federal Securities Law Guide

Responsibilities of Corporate Officers and Directors

Guide for Audit Committees

SEC Handbook

Accountants' SEC Practice Manual

SEC Accounting Rules

Federal Securities Law Reporter

GUIDE TO INTERNAL CONTROLS

Under Section 404
of the Sarbanes-Oxley Act

James Hamilton, J.D., LL.M
N. Peter Rasmussen, J.D.

CCH INCORPORATED
Chicago

books\bu\simplecovers\filename.p65

EDITORIAL STAFF

James Hamilton, J.D., LL.M.

N. Peter Rasmussen, J.D.

ISBN: 0-8080-1188-X

©2004, **CCH** INCORPORATED

4025 W. Peterson Ave.
Chicago, IL   60645-6085
1-800-248-3248
http://business.cch.com

FOREWORD

Reform of internal control of financial reporting is the centerpiece of the efforts by Congress in the Sarbanes-Oxley Act to ensure the accuracy of corporate financial statements. Section 404(a) of the Act requires a company's management to report annually on the effectiveness of the company's internal controls. In turn, the company's outside independent auditor must attest to and report on management's assessments of the internal control over financial reporting.

An effective system of internal control over financial reporting is necessary to produce reliable financial statements and other financial information used by investors. By requiring a report stating management's responsibility for the company's financial statements and internal control over financial reporting, as well as management's assessment regarding the effectiveness of such control, investors can better evaluate management's performance of its stewardship responsibilities and the financial statements themselves.

Regulation of the internal control over financial reporting has three components: Section 404, the SEC rules implementing the statute, and the Public Company Accounting Oversight Board's auditing standard complying with Section 404(b). The *Guide to Internal Controls* examines in detail all three components. In addition, the Guide includes discussion of SEC staff and PCAOB staff interpretations of the rules and standard, and reproduces the text of selected provisions.

July 2004

TABLE OF CONTENTS

CHAPTER 1—OVERVIEW

Sarbanes-Oxley Act and Internal Controls . . . . ¶ 101

SEC Rulemaking . . . . ¶ 102

Impact on Audit Committees . . . . ¶ 103

Small Business Issuers . . . . ¶ 104

Foreign Private Issuers . . . . ¶ 105

Defining Internal Controls . . . . ¶ 106

Exclusions from Requirement . . . . ¶ 107

Auditor Attestation . . . . ¶ 108

Compliance Dates . . . . ¶ 109

CHAPTER 2—MANAGEMENT REPORT ON INTERNAL CONTROLS

Introduction . . . . ¶ 201

SEC Requirements . . . . ¶ 202

Material Weakness and Significant Deficiency . . . . ¶ 203

Evaluation Methods . . . . ¶ 204

Location of Management Report . . . . ¶ 205

Transition Reports . . . . ¶ 206

Outsourcing . . . . ¶ 207

Quarterly Evaluations—Changes in Internal Controls . . . . . ¶ 208

Disclosure Controls and Procedures . . . . ¶ 209

CHAPTER 3—INTERNAL CONTROL OVER FINANCIAL REPORTING

Definition . . . . ¶ 301

Concept of Reasonable Assurance . . . . ¶ 302

Safeguarding of Corporate Assets . . . . ¶ 303

Disclosure Controls Distinguished . . . . ¶ 304

CHAPTER 4—SUITABLE FRAMEWORKS

Introduction . . . . ¶ 401

Statutory and Regulatory Background . . . . ¶ 402

COSO Background . . . . ¶ 403

COSO Framework . . . . ¶ 404

Control Environment . . . . ¶ 405

Risk Assessment . . . . ¶ 406

Control Activities . . . . ¶ 407

Information and Communication . . . . ¶ 408

Monitoring . . . . ¶ 409

Control Expectations . . . . ¶ 410

CHAPTER 5—AUDITOR ATTESTATION

Introduction . . . . ¶ 501

Overview of Standard No. 2 . . . . ¶ 502

Management's Responsibilities . . . . ¶ 503

Auditor Independence . . . . ¶ 504

Due Care . . . . ¶ 505

Materiality Considerations . . . . ¶ 506

Fraud Considerations . . . . ¶ 507

Audit Committee's Effectiveness . . . . ¶ 508

CHAPTER 6—CONTROL DEFICIENCY AND MATERIAL WEAKNESS

Control Deficiency . . . . ¶ 601

Significant Deficiency . . . . ¶ 602

Material Weakness . . . . ¶ 603

CHAPTER 7—PERFORMING AN INTERNAL CONTROL AUDIT

In General . . . . ¶ 701

Planning the Engagement . . . . ¶ 702

Evaluating Management's Assessment Process . . . . ¶ 703

Gaining Understanding of Internal Controls . . . . ¶ 704

Identifying Processes and Transactions . . . . ¶ 705

Performing Walkthroughs . . . . ¶ 706

Significant Accounts and Relevant Assertions .... ¶ 707

Identifying Controls to Test .... ¶ 708

Testing Effectiveness of Control Design .... ¶ 709

Testing Operating Effectiveness .... ¶ 710

Testing in Multiple Locations or Business Units.......... ¶ 711

CHAPTER 8—USING WORK OF OTHERS

Introduction .... ¶ 801

Evaluating Controls .... ¶ 802

Testing Work of Others............................ ¶ 803

Evaluating Fraud Risks .... ¶ 804

CHAPTER 9—FORMING OPINION ON CONTROL EFFECTIVENESS

In General .... ¶ 901

Evaluating Deficiencies .... ¶ 902

Indicator of Material Weakness .... ¶ 903

Written Representations Requirement .... ¶ 904

CHAPTER 10—RELATIONSHIP OF CONTROL AUDIT TO FINANCIAL AUDIT

Introduction .... ¶ 1001

Test of Controls (Internal Controls Audit) .... ¶ 1002

Test of Controls (Financial Statement Audit) .... ¶ 1003

Effect of Test of Controls .... ¶ 1004

Effect of Substantive Procedures .... ¶ 1005

Documentation Requirements .... ¶ 1006

CHAPTER 11—REPORTING ON INTERNAL CONTROLS

Introduction .... ¶ 1101

Auditor's Evaluation of Management Report .... ¶ 1102

Auditor's Report on Management's Assessment .... ¶ 1103

Separate Reports................................. ¶ 1104

Report Modifications .... ¶ 1105

Restrictions on Scope of Engagement .... ¶ 1106

Reference to Report of Other Auditors .... ¶ 1107

Subsequent Events .... ¶ 1108

Additional Information in Management's Report . . . . ¶ 1109

Effect of Adverse Opinion on Financial Audit . . . . ¶ 1110

Subsequent Discovery of Preexisting Information . . . . ¶ 1111

CHAPTER 12—AUDITOR'S DUTIES REGARDING SECTION 302 CERTIFICATION

Introduction . . . . ¶ 1201

Quarterly Certification . . . . ¶ 1202

Required Communication in Internal Controls Audit . . . . . ¶ 1203

No Significant Deficiencies . . . . ¶ 1204

CHAPTER 13—BANK HOLDING COMPANIES

Federal Banking Requirements . . . . ¶ 1301

Securities Law Requirements . . . . ¶ 1302

APPENDIX—SELECTED LAWS AND RULES

Sarbanes-Oxley Act Section 404 . . . . ¶ 2001

Regulation S-X Rule 2-02(f) . . . . ¶ 2002

Regulation S-K Item 308 . . . . ¶ 2003

Exchange Act Rule 13a-15 . . . . ¶ 2004

Exchange Act Rule 15d-15 . . . . ¶ 2005

Topical Index . . . . Page 161

CHAPTER 1

OVERVIEW

Sarbanes-Oxley Act and Internal Controls . . . . ¶ 101
SEC Rulemaking . . . . ¶ 102
Impact on Audit Committees . . . . ¶ 103
Small Business Issuers . . . . ¶ 104
Foreign Private Issuers . . . . ¶ 105
Defining Internal Controls . . . . ¶ 106
Exclusions from Requirement . . . . ¶ 107
Auditor Attestation . . . . ¶ 108
Compliance Dates . . . . ¶ 109

¶ 101   Sarbanes-Oxley Act and Internal Controls

On a broad level, a key aspect of management's responsibility for the preparation of financial information has been its responsibility to establish and maintain an internal control system over financial reporting. Effective internal control over financial reporting is a process designed to provide reasonable assurance regarding the reliability of financial reporting. But, since we do not live in a perfect world, effective internal control over financial reporting cannot, and does not, provide absolute assurance of achieving financial reporting objectives. (PCAOB staff interpretation of June 23, 2004.)

According to Michael Oxley, Chairman of the House Financial Services Committee, internal controls are important checks and balances in accounting and auditing system and are considered by many to the acid test for reliable financial statements.

A central goal of the Sarbanes-Oxley Act is to enhance the quality of reporting and increase investor confidence in the financial markets. Market events evidenced a need to provide investors with a clearer understanding of the processes that surround the preparation and presentation of financial information.

To enhance the quality of reporting and increase investor confidence, Sarbanes-Oxley Act Section 404(a) requires that annual reports filed with the SEC must be accompanied by a statement by company management that management is responsible for creating and maintaining adequate internal controls. In the report, management must also present its assessment of the effectiveness of those controls. Congress modeled Section 404 on a similar requirement enacted in 1991 and imposed on depository institutions through Section 36 of the Federal Deposit Insurance Act.

In addition, Section 404(b) requires the company's auditor to report on and attest to management's assessment of the company's internal controls. In requiring the registered public accounting firm preparing the audit report to attest to and report on management's assessment of internal controls, Congress does not intend for the auditor's evaluation to be the subject of a separate engagement or the basis for increased charges or fees.

¶ 102   SEC Rulemaking

The SEC adopted rules intended to accomplish the Act's goals by improving public company disclosure to investors about the extent of management's responsibility for the company's financial statements and internal control over financial reporting and the means by which management discharges its responsibility. (See Release No. 34-47986 (SEC 2003), 2003 CCH Dec., ¶ 86,923.)

The policy underlying the rules implementing Section 404 centers on the belief that the establishment and maintenance of internal control over financial reporting has always been an important responsibility of management. Moreover, an effective system of internal control over financial reporting is seen as a necessary ingredient of reliable financial statements.

By requiring a report of management stating management's responsibility for the company's financial statements and internal control over financial reporting and management's assessment regarding the effectiveness of such control, investors will be able to better evaluate management's performance of its stewardship and the reliability of a company's financial statements.

The required annual evaluation of internal control over financial reporting will also encourage companies to devote adequate resources and attention to the maintenance of such control. Additionally, the required evaluation should help to identify potential weaknesses and deficiencies in advance of a system breakdown, thereby facilitating the continuous, orderly and timely flow of information within the company and, ultimately, to investors and the marketplace.

According to the SEC, the improved disclosure is also designed to help companies detect fraudulent financial reporting earlier and perhaps thereby deter financial fraud or minimize its adverse effects. All of these benefits will increase market efficiency by improving investor confidence in the reliability of a company's financial disclosure and system of internal control over financial reporting.

The SEC rules related to Section 404 require companies, other than registered investment companies, to include in their annual reports a report of management on the company's internal control over financial reporting. The preparation of the management report on internal control over financial reporting will likely involve multiple parties, including senior management, internal auditors, in-house counsel, outside counsel and audit committee members.

¶ 103   Impact on Audit Committees

Audit committees will be impacted by the new internal controls regime. Although internal auditors are not specifically mentioned in Section 404, they have within their purview of internal control the responsibility to examine and evaluate all of a company's systems, processes, operations, functions, and activities. Thus, they are subject to a number of challenges in the Sarbanes-Oxley era.

The audit committee has a role to play in ensuring that the company has robust internal and reporting controls. The new regulatory regime helps the committee in this regard by requiring that officers assess the company's controls, and certify that they have disclosed any significant deficiencies to the audit committee. To foster additional support for internal auditors and to help meet the Act's requirements for handling complaints relating to internal controls, the head of internal audit should have a direct line of communication to the audit committee. (See remarks of SEC Commissioner Cynthia Glassman to the American Society of Corporate Secretaries, Sept. 22, 2002.)

The Sarbanes-Oxley Act requires the audit committee to be directly responsible for the appointment, compensation, and oversight of the work of the external independent auditors. The Act also requires the auditor to report on and attest to management's assessment of the company's internal controls.

Thus, internal auditors must help corporate risk officers and managers reinvigorate the risk assessment and control process over financial reporting and now, under Sarbanes-Oxley, other public disclosures. In turn, in order to be effective, internal auditors should report directly to the audit committee, in the view of some regulators, who reason that the company's entire quality assurance and monitoring program will be tainted if the internal auditors are not accountable to the audit committee. (Remarks by Federal Reserve Board Governor Susan Schmidt Bies, Institute of Internal Auditors Conference, May 7, 2003.)

In addition, the COSO Report states that the composition of a company's board and audit committee, and how the directors fulfill their duties related to the financial reporting process, are key aspects of the company's control environment. An important element of the company's internal control over financial reporting is the involvement of the board or audit committee in overseeing the financial reporting process, including assessing the reasonableness of management's accounting judgments and estimates and reviewing key filings with regulatory agencies.

Best Practice: The audit committee should actively engage the internal auditor to ensure that risk assessment and control process over financial reporting are vigorous.

Audit Committee Oversight

The question of how granular audit committee oversight over the internal control process should be is inherently difficult. Beyond the strict regulatory requirements, the clear thrust of the rules is that audit committee members need to be inquisitive, which means they should put their financial literacy to good use.

This does not mean, however, that audit committee members must re-audit the financial statements or re-design internal controls. It does mean that they should have a healthy skepticism and pursue issues until they are satisfied they have received adequate information to make an informed judgment. This is especially true with respect to instances that involve real or potential conflicts of interest for management or auditors. (See remarks of SEC Commissioner Cynthia Glassman to the American Society of Corporate Secretaries, Sept. 22, 2002.)

Best Practice: Risk-focused audit programs should be reviewed regularly to ensure audit resources are focused on the higher-risk areas as the company grows and produces and processes change. As lower-risk areas come up for review, auditors should do enough transaction testing to be confident in their risk rating. Audit committees should receive reports on all breaks in internal controls to determine where the auditing process can be strengthened. (See remarks of Federal Reserve Board Governor Susan Schmidt Bies, Institute of Internal Auditors Conference, May 7, 2003.)

In a broad sense, there is the belief that audit committees must pave the way for quality assurance over the internal audit and provide for the utmost independence, objectivity, and professionalism of the internal audit process. The audit committee sets the tone for the internal audit. (See remarks of Federal Reserve Board Governor Susan Schmidt Bies at the Conference of State Bank Supervisors, May 30, 2003.)

Line Managers

Audit committees are responsible for ensuring that their organizations have effective internal controls that are adequate to the nature and scope of their businesses and are subject to an effective audit process. According to Federal Reserve Board Governor Susan Schmidt Bies, effective internal control is the responsibility of line management. Line managers must determine the acceptable level of risk in their line of business and must assure themselves that they are getting an appropriate return for this risk and that adequate capital is being maintained.

As a best practice, Governor Bies recommends adopting a program for independently assessing the effectiveness of internal controls at least annually. Supporting functions such as accounting, internal audit, risk management, credit review, compliance, and legal should independently monitor and test the control processes to ensure that they are effective.process. The audit committee sets the tone for the internal audit. (See remarks of Federal Reserve Board Governor Susan Schmidt Bies at the Accounting Forum for Financial Institutions, June 22, 2004.)

In this sense, independent may mean that internal audit is brought in to perform something similar to an external auditor's attestation. While the details of such an approach would need to be worked out, the important point is that the audit committee should have some reasonably independent assessment of management's report. Audit committee members could use these reports to set the audit plan for the next year, to track how risks have changed and are changing within the organization, and to facilitate discussion of which controls should be added. (See remarks of Federal Reserve Board Governor Susan Schmidt Bies at the Accounting Forum for Financial Institutions, June 22, 2004.)

Independence of Internal Auditor

The issue of internal auditor independence directly involves the audit committee. The internal auditor should demonstrate independence from management and loyalty to the audit committee, and not just the appearance of independence. In turn, the audit committee should require the highest possible level of independence for the internal audit process and eliminate any threats to this independence, such as the tendency for some internal auditors to act as management consultants within the organization.

Internal auditors add value by being effective independent assessors of the quality of the internal control framework and processes. Auditors lose their independence when they perform management consulting roles for which they later will have to render an opinion. (Remarks by Federal Reserve Board Governor Susan Schmidt Bies, Institute of Internal Auditors Conference, May 7, 2003.)

Internal auditors can play a valuable role as the independent eyes and ears of the audit committee around the organization. As they work throughout the organization, they know which managers and which projects are likely to entail greater weaknesses in controls. Prompt reporting to the audit committee and timely resolution of audit findings will build credibility with the committee.

If an audit committee asks an internal auditor for recommendations on how to improve independence, the typical response should be that the test for any recommended change is whether it makes management more accountable for the ongoing effectiveness of internal controls and makes the internal audit function more effective in monitoring and process validation. (Remarks by Federal Reserve Board Governor Susan Schmidt Bies, Institute of Internal Auditors Conference, May 7, 2003.)

¶ 104   Small Business Issuers

Striking an appropriate balance regarding the needs of smaller issuers was particularly challenging for both the SEC and the PCAOB. Although the SEC's final rule implementing Sarbanes-Oxley Act Section 404 does not distinguish between large issuers and small business issuers, the Commission recognizes that many smaller issuers might encounter difficulties in evaluating their internal control over financial reporting. (See adopting release No. 34-47986 (SEC 2003), CCH Dec. ¶ 86,923.)

In this spirit, the SEC staff would support efforts by bodies such as COSO to develop an internal control framework specifically for smaller issuers. (See FAQ of June 23, 2004, Q. 16.)

Similarly, the PCAOB believes providing internal control criteria for small and medium-sized companies within the internal control framework is more appropriately within the purview of COSO.

Thus, the PCAOB's Auditing Standard No. 2 emphasizes the existing guidance within COSO as the best way of recognizing the special considerations that can and should be given to small and medium-sized companies without inappropriately weakening the standard to which these smaller entities should, nonetheless, be held. (Paragraph 15; see Release No. 34-49544 (SEC 2004), Fed. Sec. L. Rep. ¶ 87,203.) If additional tailored guidance on the internal control framework for small and medium-sized companies is needed, the Board encourages COSO, or some other appropriate body, to develop this guidance. (Paragraph E60.)

¶ 105   Foreign Private Issuers

Sarbanes-Oxley Act Section 404 makes no distinction between domestic and foreign issuers and, by its terms, clearly applies to foreign private issuers. The SEC, therefore, applies the management report on internal control over financial reporting requirement to foreign private issuers that are Exchange Act reporting companies. The SEC did, however, adopt a later compliance date for foreign private issuers.

In addition, the management of a foreign private issuer that has Exchange Act reporting obligations must also, like its domestic counterparts, report any material changes to the company's internal controls. However, because foreign private issuers are not required to file quarterly reports, the

SEC rules clarify that a foreign private issuer's management need only disclose in the annual report the material changes to its internal control over financial reporting that have occurred in the period covered by the annual report.

The management of a foreign private issuer must disclose in its annual report filed on Form 20-F or 40-F any change in its internal control over financial reporting that occurred during the period covered by the annual report and that materially affected, or is reasonably likely to affect, this internal control.

Foreign Subsidiaries

Many companies with global operations have a lag in reporting the financial results of foreign subsidiaries for financial reporting purposes. For example, a company with a December 31 year-end may consolidate the operations of foreign subsidiaries with a November 30 year-end. According to the SEC staff, this difference in period ends is acceptable in relation to the assessment of internal control over financial reporting. (See FAQ of June 23, 2004, Q. 12.)

¶ 106   Defining Internal Controls

Over the years there has been some confusion over the exact meaning and scope of the term internal control. Historically, the term was applied almost exclusively within the accounting profession. As the auditing of financial statements evolved from a process of detailed testing of transactions and account balances towards a process of sampling and testing, greater consideration of a company's internal controls became necessary in planning an audit. In 1941, the SEC adopted amendments to Rules 2-02 and 3-07 of Regulation S-X that formally codified this practice. (See Accounting Series Release No. 21, Feb. 5, 1941, 11 FR 10921.)

If an internal control component had been adequately designed, then the auditor could limit further consideration of that control to procedures to determine whether the control had been placed in operation. Accordingly, the auditor could rely on the control to serve as a basis to reduce the amount, timing or extent of substantive testing in the execution of an audit.

Conversely, if an auditor determined that an internal control component was inadequate in its design or operation, then the auditor could not rely on that control. In this instance, the auditor would conduct tests of transactions and perform additional analyses in order to accumulate sufficient, competent audit evidence to support its opinion on the financial statements.

From the outset, it was recognized that internal control is a broad concept that extends beyond the accounting functions of a company. Early attempts to define the term focused primarily on clarifying the portion of a company's internal control that an auditor should consider when planning and performing an audit of a company's financial statements. However, this did not improve the level of understanding of the term, nor satisfactorily provide the guidance sought by auditors.

In 1977, based on SEC recommendations, Congress enacted the Foreign Corrupt Practices Act, which codified the accounting control provisions contained in Statement of Auditing Standards No. 1 (codified as § 320 in the Codification of Statements on Auditing Standards). Under the FCPA, companies that have a class of securities registered under Exchange Act Section 12, or that are required to file reports under Exchange Act Section 15(d), must devise and maintain a system of internal accounting controls sufficient to provide reasonable assurances that:

● transactions are executed in accordance with management's general or specific authorization;

● transactions are recorded as necessary to permit preparation of financial statements in conformity with generally accepted accounting principles or any other criteria applicable to such statements, and to maintain accountability for assets;

● access to assets is permitted only in accordance with management's general or specific authorization; and

● the recorded accountability for assets is compared with the existing assets at reasonable intervals and appropriate action is taken with respect to any differences. See Exchange Act Section 13(b)(2).

In 1985, a private-sector initiative known as the National Commission on Fraudulent Financial Reporting, also known as the Treadway Commission, was formed to study the financial reporting system in the United States. In 1987, the Treadway Commission issued a report recommending that its sponsoring organizations work together to integrate the various internal control concepts and definitions and to develop a common reference point.

In response, the Committee of Sponsoring Organizations of the Treadway Commission (COSO) undertook an extensive study of internal control to establish a common definition that would serve the needs of companies, independent public accountants, legislators and regulatory agencies, and to provide a broad framework of criteria against which companies could evaluate the effectiveness of their internal control systems.

The Treadway Commission was sponsored by the AICPA, the American Accounting Association, the Financial Executives International (formerly Financial Executives Institute), the Institute of Internal Auditors and the Institute of Management Accountants (formerly the National Association of Accountants).

In 1992, COSO published its Internal Control—Integrated Framework. The COSO Framework defined internal control as "a process, effected by an entity's board of directors, management and other personnel, designed to provide reasonable assurance regarding the achievement of objectives" in three categories: (1) effectiveness and efficiency of operations; (2) reliability of financial reporting; and (3) compliance with applicable laws and regulations. COSO further stated that internal control consists of:

- the control environment;

- risk assessment;

- control activities;

- information and communication; and

- monitoring.

In 1996, COSO issued a supplement to its original framework to address the application of internal control over financial derivative activities.

Thus, the scope of internal control extends to policies, plans, procedures, processes, systems, activities, functions, projects, initiatives, and endeavors of all types at all levels of a company.

The COSO framework is flexible enough to work effectively at a $25 million bank or a multibillion dollar financial institution and describes how each internal control element can be tailored to smaller and less-complex organizations. (See remarks of Federal Reserve Board Governor Susan Schmidt Bies at the Accounting Forum for Financial Institutions, June 22, 2004.)

¶ 107   Exclusions from Requirement

Certain entities are exempt from the requirements of Section 404. As discussed below, these include asset-backed issuers and registered investment companies.

Asset-Backed Issuers

The SEC excluded issuers of asset-backed securities from the rules implementing Section 404. Because of their unique nature, these issuers are subject to substantially different reporting requirements. Most significantly, asset-backed issuers are generally not required to file the types of financial statements that other companies must file.

In addition, they typically are passive pools of assets without a board of directors or persons acting in a similar capacity.

Investment Companies

The internal control assessment and attestation requirements of Section 404 do not apply to registered investment companies due to an exemption found in Section 405 of the Act, and the SEC has not extended any of the requirements that would implement Section 404 to investment companies.

But note that the certification requirements implementing Section 302 of Sarbanes-Oxley do not exempt investment companies.

Thus, under the SEC rules, investment companies must maintain internal control over financial reporting. Signing officers must state that they are responsible for establishing and maintaining internal control over financial reporting, and that they have designed such internal controls, or caused them to be designed under their supervision, in order to provide reasonable assurance regarding the reliability of financial reporting and the preparation of financial statements for external purposes in accordance with generally accepted accounting principles.

The SEC also requires disclosure of any change in the investment company's internal control over financial reporting that occurred during the most recent fiscal half-year that has materially affected, or is reasonably likely to materially affect, the company's internal controls.

Signing officers must state that they have disclosed to the investment company's auditors and the audit committee all significant deficiencies and material weaknesses in the design or operation of internal control over financial reporting that are reasonably likely to adversely affect the investment company's ability to record, process, summarize, and report financial information.

¶ 108   Auditor Attestation

Complying with Sarbanes-Oxley Act Section 404(b), the PCAOB adopted Auditing Standard No. 2. (See Release No. 34-49544 (SEC 2004), FED. SEC. L. REP. ¶ 87,203.) Under the standard, the auditor's objective in an audit of internal control over financial reporting is to express an opinion on management's assessment of the effectiveness of the company's internal control over financial reporting.

To render such an opinion, the standard requires the auditor to obtain reasonable assurance about whether the company maintained, in all material respects, effective internal control over financial reporting as of the date specified in management's report. To obtain reasonable assurance, the auditor must evaluate both management's process for making its assessment and the effectiveness of internal control over financial reporting.

Although some commenters criticized the standard for going beyond the attestation required by Section 404(b), the PCAOB concluded that the approach taken in the standard is consistent with the intent of Congress. To provide the type of report at the level of assurance demanded by Sarbanes-Oxley, reasoned the Board, the auditor must evaluate both management's assessment process and the effectiveness of internal control over financial reporting. (Paragraph E12; see Release No. 34-49544 (SEC 2004), FED. SEC. L. REP. ¶ 87,203.)

For these reasons the standard refers to the attestation required by Section 404(b) as the audit of internal control over financial reporting instead of an attestation of management's assessment. The standard takes this approach both because the auditor's objective is to express an opinion on management's assessment of the effectiveness of internal control over financial reporting, just as the auditor's objective in an audit of the financial statements is to express an opinion on the fair presentation of the financials, and because the level of assurance obtained by the auditor is the same in both cases. (Paragraph E20; see Release No. 34-49544 (SEC 2004), FED. SEC. L. REP. ¶ 87,203.)

Furthermore, the standard describes an integrated audit of the financial statements and internal control over financial reporting and allows the auditor to express his or her opinions on the financial statements and on the effectiveness of internal control in separate reports or in a single, combined report.

Thus, the PCAOB believes that the expression of two opinions in all reports on management's assessment, and on the effectiveness of internal control over financial reporting, is a superior approach that balances the concerns of many different interested parties. This approach is consistent with the scope of the audit, results in more consistent reporting in differing circumstances, and makes the reports more easily understood by report users.

Use of Work of Others

Auditing Standard No. 2 allows the independent auditor to use the work of others, such as the internal auditors, but also creates an overall boundary on the use of the work of others by requiring that the auditor's own work provide the principal evidence for the audit opinion.

Auditing Standard No. 2 describes an evaluation process, focusing on the nature of the controls subject to the work of others and the competence and objectivity of the persons who performed the work, that the auditor should use in determining the extent to which he or she may use the work of others.

For example, based on the nature of the controls in the control environment, auditors should not use the work of others to reduce the amount of work they perform on the control environment. Similarly, auditors must perform walkthroughs themselves. On the other hand, the auditor could use the work of others to test controls over the period-end financial reporting process.

However, given the nature of these controls, auditors would normally determine that they should perform more of these tests themselves, and that for any of the work of others the auditors used, the degree of competence and objectivity of the individuals performing the work should be high. Therefore, the auditor might use the work of internal auditors in this area to some degree but not the work of others within the company. Because of the importance of these decisions, Auditing Standard No. 2 provides additional direction.

As mentioned, Auditing Standard No. 2 requires that, on an overall basis, the auditor's own work must provide the principal evidence for the audit opinion. Because the amount of work related to obtaining sufficient evidence to support an opinion about the effectiveness of controls is not susceptible to precise measurement, the auditor's judgment as to whether he or she has obtained the principal evidence for the opinion will be qualitative as well as quantitative.

For example, the auditor might give more weight to work performed on pervasive controls and in areas such as the control environment than on other controls such as controls over routine, low-risk transactions. Also, the work the auditor performs in the control environment and walkthroughs provide an important part of the principal evidence the auditor needs to obtain.

These principles interact to provide the auditor with considerable flexibility in using the work of others and also prevent inappropriate over-reliance on the work of others. Although Auditing Standard No. 2 requires that the auditor reperform some of the tests performed by others in order to use their work, it does not set any specific requirement on the extent of the reperformance.

For example, the standard does not require that the auditor reperform tests of controls over all significant accounts for which the auditor uses the work of others. Rather, Auditing Standard No. 2 relies on the auditor's judgment, such that the re-testing is sufficient to enable the auditor to evaluate the quality and effectiveness of the work.

The Board believes that this considerable flexibility in using the work of others should translate into a strong encouragement for companies to develop high-quality internal audit, compliance, and other such functions. The more highly competent and objective these functions are, and the more thorough their testing, the more the auditor will be able to use their work.

Evaluating Test Results

Both management and the auditor may identify deficiencies in internal control over financial reporting. A control deficiency exists when the design or operation of a control does not allow the company's management or employees, in the normal course of performing their assigned functions, to prevent or detect misstatements on a timely basis.

Auditing Standard No. 2 requires the auditor to evaluate the severity of all identified control deficiencies because such deficiencies can have an effect on the auditor's overall conclusion about whether internal control is effective. The auditor also has a responsibility to make sure that certain parties, such as the audit committee, are aware of control deficiencies that rise to a certain level of severity.

Under Auditing Standard No. 2, a control deficiency (or a combination of internal control deficiencies) should be classified as a significant deficiency if, by itself or in combination with other control deficiencies, it results in more than a remote likelihood that a misstatement in the company's annual or interim financial statements that is more than inconsequential will not be prevented or detected.

A significant deficiency should be classified as a material weakness if, by itself or in combination with other control deficiencies, it results in more than a remote likelihood that a material misstatement in the company's annual or interim financial statements will not be prevented or detected.

The definitions of significant deficiency and material weakness focus on likelihood and magnitude as the framework for evaluating deficiencies. The Board anticipates that this framework will bring increased consistency to these evaluations yet preserve an appropriate degree of judgment.

Additionally, Auditing Standard No. 2 includes examples of how these definitions would be applied in several different scenarios.

Communication to Audit Committee

Auditing Standard No. 2 requires auditors to communicate in writing to the company's audit committee all significant deficiencies and material weaknesses of which they are aware. Auditors are also required to communicate to the company's management, in writing, all control deficiencies of which they are aware that have not previously been communicated in writing to management and to notify the audit committee that such communication has been made.

Significant Deficiencies

Auditing Standard No. 2 identifies a number of circumstances that, because of their likely significant negative effect on internal control over financial reporting, are significant deficiencies as well as strong indicators that a material weakness exists.

The audit of internal control over financial reporting and the audit of the company's financial statements are an integrated activity and are required by Sarbanes-Oxley to be a single engagement. The results of the work performed in a financial statement audit provide evidence to support the auditor's conclusions on the effectiveness of internal control, and vice-versa.

Therefore, if the auditor discovers a material misstatement in the financial statements as a part of the audit of the financial statements, the auditor should consider whether internal control over financial reporting is effective. That the company's internal controls did not first detect the misstatement is, therefore, a strong indicator that the company's internal control over financial reporting is ineffective.

Timing might be a concern for some companies, particularly as it relates to making preliminary drafts of the financial statements available to the auditor. However, changes to the financial statement preparation process that increase the likelihood that the financial information is correct prior to providing it to the auditors likely will result in an improved control environment.

The auditor also must exercise judgment when performing this evaluation. For example, if the auditor initially identified a material misstatement in the financial statements but, given the circumstances, determined that management would have found the misstatement on a timely basis before the financial statements were made publicly available, the auditor might appropriately determine that the circumstance was a significant deficiency but not a material weakness.

Yet another circumstance indicating significant deficiencies as well as strong indicators that a material weakness exists is that significant deficiencies communicated to management and the audit committee have remained uncorrected after reasonable periods of time.

Significant deficiencies in internal control that are not also determined to be material weaknesses are not so severe as to require the auditor to conclude that internal control is ineffective. However, these deficiencies are, nonetheless, significant, and the auditor should expect the company to correct them.

Management's failure to correct significant deficiencies within a reasonable period of time reflects poorly on tone-at-the-top, and directly on the control environment as a whole. Additionally, the significance of the deficiency can change over time. For example, major changes in sales volume or added complexity in sales transaction structures might increase the severity of a significant deficiency affecting sales.

Forming an Opinion and Reporting

Auditing Standard No. 2 permits the auditor to express an unqualified opinion if the auditor has identified no material weaknesses in internal control after having performed all of the procedures that the auditor considers necessary in the circumstances.

In the event that the auditor cannot perform all of the procedures that the auditor considers necessary in the circumstances, Auditing Standard No. 2 permits the auditor to either qualify or disclaim an opinion. If an overall opinion cannot be expressed, Auditing Standard No. 2 requires the auditor to explain why.

Regulation S-X Rule 2-02(f) states that the attestation report on management's assessment of internal control over financial reporting must be dated, signed manually, identifying the period covered by the report and clearly stating the opinion of the accountant as to whether management's assessment of the effectiveness of the company's internal control over financial reporting is fairly stated in all material respects, or must include an opinion to the effect that an overall opinion cannot be expressed. If an overall opinion cannot be expressed, the accountant must explain why.

Auditor's Report

In addition, the auditor's report must include two opinions as a result of the audit of internal control over financial reporting: one on management's assessment and one on the effectiveness of internal control over financial reporting. The Board decided that two opinions will most clearly communicate to report readers the nature and results of the work performed and most closely track with the requirements of Sarbanes-Oxley.

The auditor's report must follow the same disclosure model as management's assessment. The SEC's final rules implementing Section 404(a) require management's assessment to disclose only material weaknesses, not significant deficiencies. Therefore, because management's assessment will disclose only material weaknesses, the auditor's report may disclose only material weaknesses.

It should be noted, however, that the SEC rules indicated that an aggregation of significant deficiencies may constitute a material weakness in a company's internal control over financial reporting, in which case disclosure would be required.

The SEC's final rules implementing Section 404(a) state that management is not permitted to conclude that the company's internal control over financial reporting is effective if there are one or more material weaknesses in the internal control over financial reporting. In other words, in such a case, management must conclude that internal control is not effective. A qualified or except for conclusion is not allowed.

Similar to the reporting of significant deficiencies, the reporting model for the auditor must follow the required reporting model for management. Therefore, because management must express an adverse conclusion if a material weakness exists, the auditor's opinion on the effectiveness of internal control over financial reporting must also be adverse. Auditing Standard No. 2 does not permit a qualified opinion in the event of a material weakness. However, Auditing Standard No. 2 also requires an opinion on management's assessment in every audit report.

In the event of a material weakness, the auditor could express an unqualified opinion on management's assessment, so long as management properly identified the material weakness and concluded in their assessment that internal control was not effective.

If the auditor and management disagree about whether a material weakness exists—for example, the auditor concludes a material weakness exists but management does not and therefore makes the conclusion in its assessment that internal control is effective—the auditor would render an adverse opinion on management's assessment.

¶ 108

The Board chose for the auditor's report to express two opinions in part because it would be more informative when a material weakness exists.

Testing Controls on Fraud

Strong internal controls provide better opportunities to detect and deter fraud. For example, many frauds resulting in financial statement restatement relied on management's ability to exploit weaknesses in internal control. To the extent that the internal control reporting required by Section 404 can help restore investor confidence by improving the effectiveness of internal controls and reducing the incidence of fraud, the auditing standard on performing the audit of internal control over financial reporting should emphasize controls that prevent or detect errors as well as fraud.

For this reason, Auditing Standard No. 2 specifically addresses and emphasizes the importance of controls over possible fraud and requires the auditor to test controls specifically intended to prevent or detect fraud that is reasonably possible to result in material misstatement of the financial statements.

In the Board's view, an attestation engagement to examine management's assessment of internal control requires the same level of work as an audit of internal control over financial reporting.

The objective of an audit of internal control over financial reporting is to form an opinion on whether management's assessment of the effectiveness of the company's internal control over financial reporting is fairly stated in all material respects. (See Regulation S-X Rule 2-02(f).)

Moreover, the Sarbanes-Oxley Act requires the auditor's report to present an evaluation of whether the internal control structure provides reasonable assurance that transactions are recorded as necessary, among other requirements. (See Section 103(a)(2)(A)(iii).)

Importantly, the auditor's conclusion will pertain directly to whether the auditor can agree with management that internal control is effective, not just to the adequacy of management's process for determining whether internal control is effective.

In the Board's view, an auditing process restricted to evaluating what management has done would not provide the auditor with a sufficiently high level of assurance that management's conclusion is correct. The auditor needs to evaluate management's assessment process to be satisfied that management has an appropriate basis for its conclusion.

The auditor, however, also needs to test the effectiveness of internal control to be satisfied that management's conclusion is correct and, therefore, fairly stated. Indeed, investors expect the independent auditor to test whether the company's internal control over financial reporting is effective, and Auditing Standard No. 2 requires the auditor to do so.

Integrated Audit

Auditing Standard No. 2 embodies an integrated standard that both: (1) addresses the work required to audit internal control over financial reporting and the relationship of that audit to the audit of the financial statements; and (2) refers to the attestation of management's assessment of the effectiveness of the internal control as the audit of internal control over financial reporting.

The Board decided that these audits should be integrated for two reasons. First, the objectives of, and work involved in performing, an audit of internal control over financial reporting and an audit of the financial statements are closely related. Second, Sarbanes-Oxley Act Section 404(b) provides that the auditor's attestation of management's assessment of internal control cannot be the subject of a separate engagement.

In addition, each audit provides the auditor with information relevant to the auditor's evaluation of the results of the other audit. For example, the auditor's discovery of misstatements in the financial statements while performing financial statement auditing procedures indicates that there may be weaknesses in the company's internal control over financial reporting. Because of the significance of this interrelationship, the Board clarified that, in order to conduct and report on the results of an audit of internal control over financial reporting pursuant to Auditing Standard No. 2, the auditor also must audit the company's financial statements.

¶ 109   Compliance Dates

A company that is an "accelerated filer," as defined in Exchange Act Rule 12b-2, must begin to comply with the management report on internal control over financial reporting requirement and the related registered public accounting firm report requirement in Items 308(a) and (b) of Regulations S-K and S-B for its first fiscal year ending on or after November 15, 2004.

A non-accelerated filer must begin to comply with these requirements for its first fiscal year ending on or after July 15, 2005.

A foreign private issuer that files its annual report on Form 20-F or Form 40-F must begin to comply with the corresponding requirements in these forms for its first fiscal year ending on or after July 15, 2005.

A company must begin to comply with the provisions of Exchange Act Rule 13a-15(d) or 15d-15(d), whichever applies, requiring an evaluation of changes to internal control over financial reporting requirements with respect to the company's first periodic report due after the first annual report that must include management's report on internal control over financial reporting.

CHAPTER 2

MANAGEMENT REPORT ON INTERNAL CONTROLS

Introduction .... ¶ 201
SEC Requirements............................. ¶ 202
Material Weakness and Significant Deficiency .... ¶ 203
Evaluation Methods .... ¶ 204
Location of Management Report.................. ¶ 205
Transition Reports............................. ¶ 206
Outsourcing .... ¶ 207
Quarterly Evaluations—Changes in Internal Controls .. ¶ 208
Disclosure Controls and Procedures .... ¶ 209

¶ 201   Introduction

The SEC believes that the purpose of internal controls and procedures for financial reporting is to ensure that companies have processes designed to provide reasonable assurance that:

● the company's transactions are properly authorized;

● its assets are safeguarded against unauthorized or improper use; and

● its transactions are properly recorded and reported. All of the above are designed to permit the preparation of the financial statements in conformity with generally accepted accounting principles.

According to Alan Beller, Director of the Division of Corporation Finance, companies will have to evaluate their internal control structures in a more thorough-going manner than has previously been the case. And the SEC rules will require new interactions between a company and its external auditors. (See remarks of Alan Beller, Director of the Division of Corporation Finance, before the American Bar Association's 2003 Conference for Corporate Counsel, June 12, 2003.)

Settlement of Enforcement Action

As part of settling an SEC enforcement action, a company consented to a permanent injunction authorizing a corporate monitor to undertake a complete overhaul of the company's corporate governance and authorizing a group of independent consultants to ascertain that the company has fully eliminated the many defects in the company's internal controls detected after a comprehensive review by the company's new outside auditors.

The company committed in advance to adopt and adhere to all corporate governance and internal control recommendations made by the Corporate Monitor and the independent consultants, subject only to appeal to the federal court that approved the settlement. The company also agreed to impose all internal controls required by Sarbanes-Oxley Act Section 404 a full year earlier than required. See *SEC v. WorldCom, Inc.* (SD NY 2003), 2003 CCH Dec. ¶ 92,456.

¶ 202   SEC Requirements

Implementing Sarbanes-Oxley Act Section 404(a), the SEC adopted rules requiring management's annual internal control report to contain the following:

● a statement of management's responsibility for establishing and maintaining adequate internal control over corporate financial reporting;

● a statement identifying the framework used by management to evaluate the effectiveness of the internal control;

● management's assessment of the effectiveness of internal control over financial reporting as of the end of the company's most recent fiscal year, including a statement as to whether or not the company's internal control over financial reporting is effective. The assessment must also disclose any material weaknesses in the internal controls identified by management; and

● a statement that the outside auditor of the company's financial statements has issued an attestation report on management's assessment of the internal control over financial reporting.

Note that management must state whether or not the company's internal control over financial reporting is effective. According to the SEC, a negative assurance statement indicating that nothing has come to management's attention to suggest that the company's internal control over financial reporting is not effective will not be acceptable.

The SEC rules do not specify the exact content of the required management report since this likely would result in boilerplate responses of little value. Rather, the SEC wants management to tailor the report to the company's circumstances.

Under the rules, management must disclose any material weakness. In addition, management will be unable to conclude that the company's internal control over financial reporting is effective if there are one or more material weaknesses in such control. Further, the framework on which management's evaluation is based will have to be a suitable, recognized control framework that is established by a body or group that has followed due-process procedures, including the broad distribution of the framework for public comment.

Commission and Staff Guidance

According to the SEC staff, even if management concludes in a report included in a timely filed Form 10-K that the company's internal control over financial reporting is not effective, the company will still be considered timely and current for purposes of Rule 144 and Forms S-2, S-3, and S-8 eligibility so long as other reporting obligations are timely satisfied. (See FAQ of June 23, 2004, Q. 4.)

SEC Deputy Chief Accountant Scott Taub has advised that the company is responsible for designing and implementing the system of internal controls. It must maintain records to ensure that transactions are appropriately recorded, the internal control system is effectively administered and the financial statements are prepared in accordance with GAAP. He emphasized that documentation is required and is the responsibility of management. (See remarks of Scott Taub, Deputy Chief Accountant at the University of Southern California's Leventhal School of Accounting, May 29, 2003.)

Management must evaluate the effectiveness of the controls based on procedures sufficient to evaluate their design and to test their operating effectiveness. Complete reliance on external auditors is not appropriate, he cautioned. Management must make the final decisions, exercise its own judgment in performing the analysis and oversee the work that is done. He noted, for example, that outsourcing a major part of the work to the auditors would not be appropriate, nor would reliance on the auditors to determine which tests to perform, or to provide software that determines the effectiveness of controls. (See remarks of Scott Taub, Deputy Chief Accountant at the University of Southern California's Leventhal School of Accounting, May 29, 2003.)

Similarly, SEC Commissioner Cynthia Glassman addressed the question of how deeply involved independent auditors could be in the implementation of internal controls and still maintain their independence. She concluded that, while auditors must assess internal controls as part of their audit, and while they can generally assist management, the design and implementation of internal controls must remain management's responsibility. (See remarks of Commissioner Cynthia Glassman before the Exchequer Club, July 16, 2003.)

Throughout the attestation process, the auditors must be independent, which means they cannot have usurped management's responsibilities, or be reviewing their own work. Commissioner Glassman emphasized that it is not

¶ **202**

appropriate for an auditor to condition the attestation on the use of a proprietary software package or other services offered by the auditor.

Auditor Attestation

The SEC rules also require a company to file, as part of its annual report, the attestation report of the registered public accounting firm that audited the company's financial statements.

Auditor Independence Issues

The SEC recognizes that, because the independent auditor must attest to management's assessment of internal control over financial reporting, management and the auditors will need to coordinate their processes of documenting and testing the internal controls.

But companies and their auditors must remember that SEC rules on auditor independence prohibit an auditor from providing certain nonaudit services to an audit client. Auditors may assist management in documenting internal controls, but when the auditor is engaged to assist management in documenting internal controls, management must be actively involved in the process.

Cautionary Note: While understanding of the need for coordination between management and the auditor, the SEC cautions that management cannot delegate its responsibility to assess its internal controls over financial reporting to the auditor. Management's acceptance of responsibility for the documentation and testing performed by the auditor does not satisfy the auditor independence rules.

¶ 203   Material Weakness and Significant Deficiency

In assessing the effectiveness of the internal controls, management must include disclosure of any identified material weaknesses in the company's internal control over financial reporting. According to the SEC, management is not permitted to conclude that the company's internal control over financial reporting is effective if there are one or more material weaknesses in the company's internal control over financial reporting.

The SEC rules thus provide a threshold for concluding that a company's internal controls are effective in that management is precluded from determining that a company's internal controls are effective if it identifies one or more material weaknesses in them.

The rules also specify that management's report must include disclosure of any material weakness in the company's internal control identified by management in the course of its evaluation.

The terms material weakness and significant deficiency both represent deficiencies in the design or operation of internal control that could adversely affect a company's ability to record, process, summarize and report financial data consistent with the assertions of management in the company's financial statements, with a material weakness constituting a greater deficiency than a significant deficiency. It is the SEC's view, that an aggregation of significant deficiencies could constitute a material weakness in a company's internal control over financial reporting.

While all material weaknesses must be identified and disclosed, management is not obligated to disclose the existence or nature of identified significant deficiencies. However, if management identifies a significant deficiency that, when combined with other significant deficiencies, is determined to be a material weakness, management must disclose the material weakness and, to the extent material to an understanding of the disclosure, the nature of the significant deficiencies. (See FAQ of June 23, 2004, Q. 11.)

In addition, if a material change is made to either disclosure controls and procedures or to internal controls in response to a significant deficiency, the company must disclose the change and should consider whether it is necessary to discuss further the nature of the significant deficiency in order to render the disclosure not misleading. (See FAQ of June 23, 2004, Q. 11.)

Note also that an outside auditor aware of a significant deficiency must communicate the significant deficiency to the audit committee as required by PCAOB Auditing Standard No. 2.

Definitions

In its adopting release for the rules implementing Section 404, the Commission expressed an intention to incorporate the definitions of "significant deficiency" and "material weakness" as they exist in the standards used by auditors of public companies. (Release No. 34-47986 (SEC 2003), 2003 CCH Dec. ¶ 86,923.) Looking to the definitions as revised by the PCAOB is consistent with this intention and, accordingly, the SEC staff will apply the PCAOB definitions in interpreting the Commission rules in this area. (See FAQ of June 23, 2004, Q. 13.)

In Auditing Standard No. 2, the PCAOB defines a "significant deficiency" as a control deficiency, or combination of control deficiencies, that adversely affects the company's ability to initiate, authorize, record, process, or report external financial data reliably in accordance with generally accepted accounting principles such that there is more than a remote likelihood that a misstatement of the company's annual or interim financial statements that is more than inconsequential will not be prevented or detected. (Paragraph 9; see Release No. 34-49544 (SEC 2004), FED. SEC. L. REP. ¶ 87,203.)

The Board defines a "material weakness" as a significant deficiency, or combination of significant deficiencies, that results in more than a remote likelihood that a material misstatement of the annual or interim financial statements will not be prevented or detected. (Paragraph 10; see Release No. 34-49544 (SEC 2004), FED. SEC. L. REP. ¶ 87,203.)

For a more complete discussion of these definitions, see ¶ 602 and ¶ 603.

Staff Guidance

Under the SEC rules, management may not conclude that a company's internal control over financial reporting is effective if a material weakness exists in its internal control over financial reporting.

Similarly, the SEC staff has indicated that management may not qualify its conclusions. For example, management cannot state that controls and procedures are effective except to the extent that certain problems have been identified. Rather, management must take those problems into account when concluding whether the company's internal control over financial reporting is effective. Management may state however, that controls are ineffective for specific reasons. (See FAQ of June 23, 2004, Q. 5.)

On a separate issue, the staff said that, if management's report on internal control over financial reporting does not identify a material weakness but the accountant's attestation report does, or vice versa, this situation does not constitute a disagreement between the company and the auditor that must be reported pursuant to Regulation S-K Item 304. However, such differences in identification of material weaknesses could trigger other disclosure obligations. (See FAQ of June 23, 2004, Q. 6.)

¶ 204   Evaluation Methods

Since the methods of conducting evaluations of internal control over financial reporting will vary from company to company, the SEC does not specify the method or procedures to be performed in an evaluation.

In conducting an evaluation and developing an assessment of the effectiveness of internal controls, however, a company must maintain evidential matter, including documentation, to provide reasonable support for management's assessment of the effectiveness of the company's internal controls. The SEC considers developing and maintaining such evidential matter to be an inherent element of effective internal controls and the rules remind companies to maintain such evidential matter.

The assessment of a company's internal control over financial reporting must be based on procedures sufficient both to evaluate its design and to test its operating effectiveness. Controls subject to such assessment include, but are not limited to:

● controls over initiating, recording, processing and reconciling account balances, classes of transactions and disclosure and related assertions included in the financial statements;

● controls related to the initiation and processing of non-routine and
non-systematic transactions;

● controls related to the selection and application of appropriate
accounting policies;

● and controls related to the prevention, identification, and detection of fraud.

The nature of a company's testing activities will largely depend on the
circumstances of the company and the significance of the control.

But note that inquiry alone generally will not provide an adequate basis
for management's assessment. This does not mean that management person-
ally must conduct the necessary activities to evaluate the design and test the
operating effectiveness of the company's internal controls. Activities, including those necessary to provide management with the information on which it
bases its assessment, may be conducted by non-management personnel acting
under the supervision of management.

Assistance of Auditor

The company's auditor may provide limited assistance to management in
documenting internal controls and making recommendations for changes to
internal controls. The SEC staff has cautioned, however, that management has
the ultimate responsibility for the assessment, documentation and testing of
the company's internal controls over financial reporting. (See FAQ of June 23,
2004, Q. 17.)

¶ 205   Location of Management's Report

Although the SEC rules do not specify where management's internal
control report must appear in the company's annual report, the Commission
said the report should be in close proximity to the corresponding attestation
report issued by the company's public accounting firm. The SEC expects that
many companies will choose to place the internal control report and attestation report near the companies' MD&A disclosure or in a portion of the
document immediately preceding the financial statements.

¶ 206   Transition Reports

A company must provide management's report on internal control over financial reporting, and the related auditor attestation report, when filing a transition report on Form 10-K. (See FAQ of June 23, 2004, Q. 8.)

Because transition reports filed on Form 10-K must contain audited financial statements, the SEC staff reasoned that they must also include management's report on internal control, subject to the transition provisions specified in Release No. 34-47986, Fed. Sec. L. Rep., 2003 CCH Dec. ¶ 86,923. The transition provisions relating to management's report on internal control should be applied to the transition period as if it were a fiscal year. Transition reports on Form 10-Q need not include a management report on internal control.

¶ 207   Outsourcing

Companies often rely on third party service providers to perform certain functions where the outsourced activity affects the initiation, authorization, recording, processing or reporting of transactions in the financial statements, such as payroll.

While management maintains a responsibility to assess the controls over the outsourced operations, the SEC staff advises that management would be able to rely on a Type 2 SAS 70 performed by the auditors of the third party service providers. Moreover, management can so rely even if the auditors of the third party service provider are the same as the auditors of the company. Further, management would be able to rely on a Type 2 SAS 70 report on the service provider that is as of a different year-end. (See FAQ of June 23, 2004, Q. 14.)

Note, however, that management is still responsible for maintaining and evaluating, as appropriate, controls over the flow of information to and from the service organization.

In addition, the staff has cautioned that, if management were to engage the company's audit firm to also prepare the Type 2 SAS 70 report on the service organization, management would not be able to rely on that report for purposes of internal control over financial reporting. (See FAQ of June 23, 2004, Q. 14.)

The question of how current a Type 2 SAS 70 report must be before management can rely on it as evidence of the effectiveness of internal controls at a service organization has been addressed by the PCAOB staff, which refers to portions of the standard providing directions when a significant period of time has elapsed between the period covered by the tests of controls in the service auditor's report and the date of management's assessment.

(Paragraphs B25 through B27; see Release No. 34-49544 (SEC 2004), FED. SEC. L. REP. ¶ 87,203.)

These directions do not establish any bright lines since their application does not result in a precise answer as to whether a service auditor's report issued more than six months prior to the date of management's assessment is not current enough to provide any evidence. Rather, the directions state that, when a significant period of time has elapsed between the time period covered by the tests of controls in the service auditor's report and the date of management's assessment, additional procedures should be performed.

Paragraph B26 provides directions to the auditor in determining whether to obtain additional evidence about the operating effectiveness of controls at the service organization. The auditor's procedures to obtain additional evidence will typically be more extensive the longer the period of time that has elapsed between the time period covered by the service auditor's report and the date of management's assessment. (See staff interpretation of June 23, 2004, Q. 25.)

Also, those auditor's procedures will vary depending on the importance of the controls at the service organization to management's assessment and on the level of interaction between the company's controls and the controls at the service organization.

The auditor's procedures will be focused on, among other things, identifying changes in the service organization's controls subsequent to the period covered by the service auditor's report. The auditor should be alert for situations in which management has not made changes to its procedures and controls to respond to changes in procedures and controls at the service organization. These situations might result in errors not being prevented or detected in a timely manner.

The PCAOB staff will allow a registered public accounting firm doing an integrated audit of an issuer to obtain evidence from a service auditor's report issued by a non-registered public accounting firm. (See staff interpretation of June 23, 20004, Q. 26.)

Paragraph B24 of Auditing Standard No. 2 directs the auditor to make inquiries concerning the service auditor's reputation, competence, and independence in determining whether the service auditor's report provides sufficient evidence to support management's assessment and the auditor's opinion on internal control over financial reporting. (See Release No. 34-49544 (SEC 2004), FED. SEC. L. REP. ¶ 87,203.) But it does not require that the service auditor be a registered public accounting firm.

However, the PCAOB staff reminds the auditor to be aware of how evidence obtained from a service auditor's report issued by a non-registered firm interacts with the Board's registration rules.

Any public accounting firm that plays a substantial role in the preparation of an audit report must register with the Board. Because of the nature of the service auditor's report, when a registered public accounting firm obtains evidence from a service auditor's report in the audit of an issuer, the service auditor has participated in the audit of the issuer. If the service auditor's work, measured in terms of either services or procedures, meets the "substantial role" threshold as defined in Rule 1001(p)(ii)) for the audit of the user organization, the service auditor must be registered with the Board. (See staff interpretation of June 23, 2004, Q. 26.)

¶ 208   Quarterly Evaluations—Changes in Internal Controls

As a general principle, the SEC believes that each company should have the flexibility to design its system of internal controls to fit its particular circumstances. The management of each company should perform evaluations of the design and operation of the company's entire system of internal control over financial reporting over a period of time that is adequate for it to determine whether, as of the end of the company's fiscal year, the design and operation of the company's internal control over financial reporting are effective

With this in mind, the SEC dropped its demand for quarterly evaluations of internal controls as extensive as the annual evaluation. Instead, the Commission requires a company's management, with the participation of the principal executive and financial officers, to evaluate any change in the company's internal controls that occurred during a fiscal quarter that has materially affected, or is reasonably likely to materially affect, the company's internal control over financial reporting.

A company must disclose any change in its internal control over financial reporting that occurred during the fiscal quarter covered by the quarterly report, or the last fiscal quarter in the case of an annual report, that has materially affected, or is reasonably likely to materially affect, the company's internal controls.

Although the rules do not expressly require the company to disclose the reasons for any change that occurred during a fiscal quarter, or to otherwise elaborate about the change, a company will have to determine, on a facts and circumstances basis, whether the reasons for the change, or other information about the circumstances surrounding the change, constitute material information necessary to make the disclosure about the change not misleading under the antifraud rule.

A company need not disclose changes or improvements to controls made as a result of preparing for its first management report on internal control over financial reporting. If the company were to identify a material weakness, however, it should carefully consider whether that fact should be disclosed, as well as changes made in response to the material weakness. (See FAQ of June 23, 2004, Q. 9.)

After the first management report on internal control over financial reporting, pursuant to Regulation S-K Item 308, the company must identify and disclose any material changes in its internal control over financial reporting in each quarterly and annual report. This would encompass disclosing a change to internal control over financial reporting that was not necessarily in response to an identified significant deficiency or material weakness (i.e., the implementation of a new information system) if it materially affected the internal control over financial reporting.

Materiality, as with all materiality judgments in this area, would be determined on the basis of the impact on internal control over financial reporting and the materiality standard articulated in U.S. Supreme Court opinions.

In general, information is material under federal securities law if a reasonable investor would consider it important in making an investment decision. Materiality therefore depends on the significance that a reasonable investor would place on the misrepresented or withheld information. There must be a substantial likelihood that, under all the circumstances, the misstated or omitted fact would have assumed actual significance in a reasonable investor's investment decision. Stated differently, there must be a substantial likelihood that reasonable investors would have viewed disclosure of the fact omitted or misrepresented as having significantly altered the "total mix" of information made available. *TSC Industries, Inc. v. Northway, Inc.* (US Sup. Ct. 1976), 1976-77 CCH Dec. ¶ 95,615; *Basic, Inc. v. Levinson* (US Sup. Ct. 1988), 1987-88 CCH Dec. ¶ 93,645.

This would also include disclosing a change to internal control over financial reporting related to a business combination for which the acquired entity that has been or will be excluded from an annual management report on internal control over financial reporting. As an alternative to ongoing disclosure for such changes in internal control over financial reporting, a company may choose to disclose all such changes to internal control over financial reporting in the annual report in which its assessment that encompasses the acquired business is included.

¶ 209   Disclosure Controls and Procedures

Although an evaluation of the effectiveness of disclosure controls and procedures must be undertaken quarterly, the SEC expects that for purposes of disclosure by domestic companies, the traditional relationship between disclosure in annual reports on Form 10-K and intervening quarterly reports on Form 10-Q will continue. Disclosure in an annual report that remains accurate need not be repeated. Rather, disclosure in quarterly reports may make appropriate reference to disclosures in the most recent annual report, and where appropriate intervening quarterly reports, and disclose subsequent developments required to be disclosed in the quarterly report.

Evaluation of disclosure controls and procedures and internal control over financial reporting in respect of compliance with applicable laws or regulations does intersect at certain points, including, for example, whether the company has controls to ensure that the effects of non-compliance with laws, rules and regulations are recorded in the its financial statements, including the recognition of probable losses under FASB Statement No. 5, Accounting for Contingencies.

While the definition of internal control over financial reporting does not encompass laws and rules outside those regulating the preparation of financial statements, the SEC staff has advised corporate managers that, as part of their evaluation of a disclosure controls and procedures, they must appropriately consider the company's compliance with other laws, rules and regulations, such as rules requiring disclosure of the existence of a code of ethics pursuant to Sarbanes-Oxley. (See FAQ of June 23, 2004, Q. 10.)

Such consideration should include assessing whether the company: (1) adequately monitors such compliance; and (2) has appropriate disclosure controls and procedures to ensure that required disclosure of legal or regulatory matters is provided.

Disclosure to Audit Committee

The SEC expects, however, that as certifying officers become aware of a significant deficiency, material weakness or fraud requiring disclosure outside of the formal evaluation process or after the management's most recent evaluation of internal control over financial reporting, they will disclose it to the company's auditors and audit committee.

CHAPTER **3**

INTERNAL CONTROL OVER FINANCIAL REPORTING

Definition . . . . ¶ 301
Concept of Reasonable Assurance . . . . ¶ 302
Safeguarding of Corporate Assets . . . . ¶ 303
Disclosure Controls Distinguished . . . . ¶ 304

¶ 301   Definition

The SEC rules and PCAOB Auditing Standard No. 2 contain essentially the same definition for "internal control over financial reporting." The SEC defines the term to mean a process designed by, or under the supervision of, the principal executive and principal financial officers, or persons performing similar functions, and effected by the board of directors, management and other personnel, to provide reasonable assurance regarding the reliability of financial reporting and the preparation of financial statements for external purposes in accordance with generally accepted accounting principles and includes those policies and procedures that:

● pertain to the maintenance of records that in reasonable detail accurately and fairly reflect the company's transactions and dispositions of assets;

● provide reasonable assurance that transactions are recorded as necessary to permit preparation of financial statements in accordance with generally accepted accounting principles, and corporate receipts and expenditures are being made only in accordance with authorizations of management and directors; and

● provide reasonable assurance regarding prevention or timely detection of unauthorized acquisition, use or disposition of corporate assets that could have a material effect on the financial statements.

According to the SEC, the scope of the term "preparation of financial statements in accordance with generally accepted accounting principles" used in the definition encompasses financial statements prepared for regulatory reporting purposes.

The two elements of the definition dealing with maintenance of records and providing assurance that transactions are recorded were inserted to clarify that management's report on internal controls, to which the company's public accounting firm will have to attest and report, specifically covers the matters referenced in Sarbanes-Oxley Act Section 103.

Section 103 requires the PCAOB to include in the auditing standards that it adopts, among other things:

● a requirement that each public accounting firm describe in each audit report the scope of its testing of the company's internal control structure and procedures performed in fulfilling its internal control evaluation and reporting required by Sarbanes-Oxley Act Section 404(b);

● present in the audit report (or attestation report) its findings from such testing, as well as an evaluation of whether the company's internal control structure and procedures:

(1) include maintenance of records that in reasonable detail accurately and fairly reflect the transactions and dispositions of the company's assets; and

(2) provide reasonable assurance that transactions are recorded as necessary to permit preparation of financial statements in accordance with generally accepted accounting principles, and that receipts and expenditures of the company are being made only in accordance with the authorization of management and directors of the company.

In the audit report (or attestation report), the public accounting firm also must describe, at a minimum, material weaknesses in such internal controls and any material noncompliance found on the basis of such testing.

¶ 302   Concept of Reasonable Assurance

It can be seen that the concept of "reasonable assurance" has been built into the Sarbanes-Oxley Act and the definition of "internal control over financial reporting" and is also integral to the auditor's opinion. In addition, management's assessment of the effectiveness of internal control over financial reporting is expressed at the level of reasonable assurance.

Reasonable assurance includes the understanding that there is a remote likelihood that material misstatements will not be prevented or detected on a timely basis. Although not absolute assurance, reasonable assurance is, nevertheless, a high level of assurance. (Paragraph 17 of Auditing Standard No. 2; see Release No. 34-49544 (SEC 2004), FED. SEC. L. REP. ¶ 87,203.)

That said, regulators recognize that there are limitations on the amount of assurance the auditor can obtain as a result of performing the audit of internal control over financial reporting. Such limitations arise because an audit is conducted on a test basis and requires the exercise of professional judgment.

Nevertheless, the audit of internal control over financial reporting includes obtaining an understanding of the internal controls, testing and evaluating their design and operating effectiveness, and performing such other procedures as the auditor considers necessary to obtain reasonable assurance about whether the internal controls are effective. (Paragraph 18 of Auditing Standard No. 2; see Release No. 34-49544 (SEC 2004), FED. SEC. L. REP. ¶ 87,203.)

But note that the auditor's report on internal control over financial reporting does not relieve management of its responsibility for assuring users of its financial reports about the effectiveness of internal control over financial reporting.

Finally, it should be remembered that there is no difference in the level of work performed or assurance obtained by the auditor when expressing an opinion on management's assessment of effectiveness or when expressing an opinion directly on the effectiveness of internal control over financial reporting.

In either case, auditors must obtain sufficient evidence to provide a reasonable basis for their opinion and the use and evaluation of management's assessment is inherent in expressing either opinion. (Paragraph 19 of Auditing Standard No. 2; see Release No. 34-49544 (SEC 2004), FED. SEC. L. REP. ¶ 87,203.)

¶ 303   Safeguarding of Corporate Assets

Another important element of the definition makes explicit reference to assurances regarding use or disposition of the company's assets. This provision was included to make clear that the safeguarding of the company's assets is one of the elements of internal control over financial reporting.

Safeguarding of assets had long been a primary objective of internal accounting control. In 1988, Statement of Auditing Standards No. 55 (codified as AU 319 in the Codification of Statements on Auditing Standards), revised the definition of internal control and expanded auditors' responsibilities for considering internal control in a financial statement audit.

The prior classification of internal control into the two categories of internal accounting control and administrative control was replaced with the single term internal control structure, which consisted of three interrelated components—control environment, the accounting system, and control procedures. Under this new definition, the safeguarding of assets was no longer a primary objective, but a subset of the control procedures component.

The COSO Report followed this shift in the iteration of safeguarding of assets, stating that operations objectives "pertain to effectiveness and efficiency of the entity's operations, including performance and profitability goals and safeguarding resources against loss." (See COSO "Addendum to Reporting to External Parties," Internal Control-Integrated Framework (1994), at p. 154.)

The COSO report, however, also clarifies that safeguarding of assets can fall within other categories of internal control depending on the circumstances. For example, according to COSO, controls to prevent theft of assets—such as maintaining a fence around inventory and a gatekeeper verifying proper authorization of requests for movement of goods—fall under the operations category. These controls normally would not be relevant to the reliability of financial statement preparation, because any inventory losses would be detected pursuant to periodic physical inspection and recorded in the financial statements. However, if for financial reporting purposes management relies solely on perpetual inventory records, as may be the case for interim reporting, the physical security controls would then also fall within the financial reporting category because they would be needed to ensure reliable financial reporting. (See COSO "Addendum to Reporting to External Parties," Internal Control-Integrated Framework (1994), at p. 37.)

The 1994 addendum was issued in response to a concern expressed by some parties, including the General Accounting Office, that the management reports contemplated by the COSO Report did not adequately address controls relating to safeguarding of assets and therefore would not fully respond to the requirements of the FCPA.

In the addendum, COSO concluded that while it believed its definition of internal control in its 1992 report remained appropriate, it recognized that the FCPA encompasses certain controls related to safeguarding of assets and that there is a reasonable expectation on the part of some readers of management's internal control reports that the reports will cover such controls.

The addendum therefore defines the term "internal control over safeguarding of assets against unauthorized acquisition, use or disposition" to be a process, effected by a company's board of directors, management and other personnel, designed to provide reasonable assurance regarding prevention or timely detection of unauthorized acquisition, use or disposition of the entity's assets that could have a material effect on the financial statements.

In order to achieve the desired result and to provide consistency with COSO's 1994 addendum, the SEC incorporated this definition into its definition of internal control over financial reporting since the definition will be used for purposes of public management reporting, and the companies subject to Section 404 are also subject to the FCPA. This is why safeguarding of assets as provided is specifically included in the SEC's definition of internal control over financial reporting.

According to PCAOB Auditing Standard No. 2, material weaknesses relating to controls over the safeguarding of assets would only exist when the company does not have effective controls (considering both safeguarding and other controls) to prevent or detect a material misstatement of the financial statements. (Paragraph C4; see Release No. 34-49544 (SEC 2004), FED. SEC. L. REP. ¶ 87,203.)

¶ 304   Disclosure Controls Distinguished

There has been some confusion as to the differences between a company's disclosure controls and procedures and a company's internal control over financial reporting. Exchange Act Rule 13a-15(d) defines "disclosure controls and procedures" to mean controls and procedures designed to ensure that information required to be disclosed by the company in the reports that it files or submits under the Exchange Act is recorded, processed, summarized and reported, within SEC-specified time periods.

The definition further states that disclosure controls and procedures include controls and procedures designed to ensure that the information required to be disclosed by a company in the reports that it files or submits is accumulated and communicated to the company's management, including its principal executive and principal financial officers, as appropriate to allow timely decisions regarding required disclosure.

Although there is substantial overlap between a company's disclosure controls and procedures and its internal controls, the SEC has admitted, there are some elements of disclosure controls and procedures that are not subsumed by internal controls and some elements of internal controls that are not subsumed by the definition of disclosure controls and procedures.

The broad COSO description of internal controls, which includes the efficiency and effectiveness of a company's operations and the company's compliance with laws and regulations (not restricted to the federal securities laws), would not be wholly subsumed within the definition of disclosure controls and procedures.

Some components of internal control over financial reporting will be included in disclosure controls and procedures for all companies. In particular, disclosure controls and procedures will include those components of internal control that provide reasonable assurances that transactions are recorded as necessary to permit preparation of financial statements in accordance with generally accepted accounting principles. However, in designing their disclosure controls and procedures, companies can be expected to make judgments regarding the processes on which they will rely to meet applicable requirements.

In doing so, some companies might design their disclosure controls and procedures so that certain components of internal control over financial reporting pertaining to the accurate recording of transactions and disposition of assets or to the safeguarding of assets are not included. For example, a company might have developed internal controls that include as a component of safeguarding of assets dual signature requirements or limitations on signature authority on checks. That company could nonetheless determine that this component is not part of disclosure controls and procedures.

The SEC believes that, while there is substantial overlap between internal controls and disclosure controls and procedures, many companies will design their disclosure controls and procedures so that they do not include all components of internal control over financial reporting.

SEC rules require quarterly evaluations of disclosure controls and procedures and disclosure of the conclusions regarding effectiveness of disclosure controls and procedures. These evaluation and disclosure requirements will continue to apply to disclosure controls and procedures, including the elements of internal control over financial reporting that are subsumed within disclosure controls and procedures.

As stated, the SEC requires quarterly evaluation of the effectiveness of disclosure controls and procedures. While the evaluation is of effectiveness overall, a company's management has the ability to make judgments that evaluations, particularly quarterly evaluations, should focus on developments since the most recent evaluation, areas of weakness or continuing concern or other aspects of disclosure controls and procedures that merit attention.

Finally, the nature of the quarterly evaluations of those components of internal control over financial reporting that are subsumed within disclosure controls and procedures should be informed by the purposes of disclosure controls and procedures.

For example, where a component of internal control over financial reporting is subsumed within disclosure controls and procedures, even where systems testing of that component would clearly be required as part of the annual evaluation of internal controls, management could make a different determination of the appropriate nature of the evaluation of that component for purposes of a quarterly evaluation of disclosure controls and procedures.

Foreign Private Issuers

SEC rules require the management of a foreign private issuer to evaluate and disclose conclusions regarding the effectiveness of its disclosure controls and procedures only in the annual report and not on a quarterly basis. The primary reason for this treatment is because foreign private issuers are not subject to mandated quarterly reporting requirements under the Exchange Act.

CHAPTER **4**

SUITABLE FRAMEWORKS

Introduction . . . . ¶ 401
Statutory and Regulatory Background . . . . ¶ 402
COSO Background . . . . ¶ 403
COSO Framework . . . . ¶ 404
Control Environment . . . . ¶ 405
Risk Assessment . . . . ¶ 406
Control Activities . . . . ¶ 407
Information and Communication . . . . ¶ 408
Monitoring . . . . ¶ 409
Control Expectations . . . . ¶ 410

¶ 401   Introduction

SEC rules specify that management must base its evaluation of the effectiveness of the company's internal control over financial reporting on a suitable, recognized control framework that is established by a body or group that has followed due-process procedures, including the broad distribution of the framework for public comment.

The Commission believes that the use of standard measures will enhance the quality of the internal control report and promote the comparability of the internal control reports of different companies. The rules require management's report to identify the evaluation framework employed to assess the effectiveness of the company's internal control over financial reporting.

The SEC is aware that some of the evaluation frameworks used to assess a foreign company's internal controls in its home country do not require a statement regarding whether the company's system of internal control has been effective. Under the rules, management of a foreign reporting company who relies on such an evaluation framework used in its home country is nevertheless under an obligation to state affirmatively whether its company's internal controls are effective.

¶ 402   Statutory and Regulatory Background

Sarbanes-Oxley Act Section 404 requires annual reports to be accompanied by a statement from management assessing the effectiveness of the company's internal. In addition, the company's auditor must report on and attest to managements assessment of the company's internal controls. The statute provides that the auditor's attestation will be made in accordance with standards adopted by the PCAOB but does not specify any framework or methodology for the underlying assessment.

In the proposed rules under Section 404 (see Release No. 33-8138 (SEC 2002), 2002 CCH Dec. ¶ 86,733), the SEC did not identify any particular framework for assessing the effectiveness of internal controls. The proposed rules were fairly open-ended and provided management with significant flexibility in determining the appropriate framework for the evaluation of internal controls. The proposing release stated that the proposed amendments "do not specify the exact content of the proposed management report, as this likely would result in boilerplate responses of little value." "We believe that management should tailor the report to the company's circumstances," stated the agency.

Several commenters suggested that the final rules should include more a more specific definition of an acceptable analytical framework. As described by Scott Taub, the SEC's deputy chief accountant, in remarks delivered in May 2003, commenters were concerned that "requiring an evaluation of controls without specifying the criteria on which to evaluate them would be like a requirement that financial statements be fair, without any GAAP on which to rely in evaluating fairness." (See remarks at the University of Southern California's Levanthal School of Accounting, May 29, 2003.)

Some commenters suggested the adoption of a particular framework, such as that set forth in the report of the Committee of Sponsoring Organizations of the Treadway Commission, or COSO. Others urged the SEC to acknowledge the COSO framework as being suitable for purposes of managements evaluation, while some commenters suggested that the SEC should require management to evaluate the effectiveness of a company's internal control over financial reporting using suitable control criteria established by a group that follows due process procedures.

For example, the American Institute of Certified Public Accountants stated that the SEC should require management to assess the effectiveness of the company's internal control over financial reporting using suitable, recognized control criteria established through due process. "Requiring the use of suitable criteria established by groups composed of experts that follow due-process procedures would provide benefits to users and to regulators similar to the benefits achieved by requiring the use of Generally Accepted Accounting Principles in the preparation of financial statements," stated the AICPA.

The association added that the use of such criteria would permit comparability among reporting entities. In addition, such established criteria are available publicly and thus easily accessible to users. The institute urged the SEC to acknowledge that the criteria set forth in the COSO report meet these conditions.

KPMG LLP wrote that it would be difficult "for individual entities or non-accounting industry trade groups to secure the necessary expertise and resources to develop suitable internal control criteria." The accounting firm also stated that bodies such as COSO are more likely to maintain and update their criteria as conditions change and additional needs arise.

In the final rules, the SEC declined to require the use of any particular analytical structure. As adopted, the rules provide that the framework on which management's evaluation of the issuer's internal control over financial reporting "is based must be a suitable, recognized control framework that is established by a body or group that has followed due-process procedures, including the broad distribution of the framework for public comment."

A suitable framework under the SEC rule would consist of a group of standards and clearly-defined criteria for use in the required assessments. According to the SEC, such a suitable framework must: (1) be free from bias; (2) permit reasonably consistent qualitative and quantitative measurements of a company's internal control; (3) be sufficiently complete so that those relevant factors that would alter a conclusion about the effectiveness of a company's internal controls are not omitted; and (4) be relevant to an evaluation of internal control over financial reporting.

In the adopting release, the SEC stated that management's report on the effectiveness of internal control must identify the evaluation framework used to assess the company's internal control over financial reporting. The Commission specifically endorsed the COSO framework, stating that the COSO structure "satisfies our criteria and may be used as an evaluation framework for purposes of management's annual internal control evaluation and disclosure requirements." The agency also concluded that the Guidance on Assessing Control published by the Canadian Institute of Chartered Accountants and the Turnbull Report published by the Institute of Chartered Accountants in England and Wales would also be suitable frameworks. Noting that these other acceptable evaluation standards exist outside of the United States and that frameworks other than COSO may be developed within the United States in the future that satisfy the intent of the statute without diminishing the benefits to investors, the Commission declined to require the use of this particular structure.

In the final audit standard adopted by the PCAOB concerning audits of internal controls over financial reporting pursuant to Section 404, the board based its performance and reporting directions on the COSO internal control framework. According to the PCAOB, it used the COSO framework because of the frequency with which management of public companies are expected to use that framework for their assessments. Recognizing that other suitable frameworks have been published in other countries that may not contain exactly the same elements as COSO, the PCAOB stated that these alternate frameworks should have elements that encompass all of COSO's general themes.

¶ 403   COSO Background

The COSO framework has its roots in the National Commission on Fraudulent Financial Reporting. The commission was an independent private-sector initiative jointly sponsored and funded by the American Accounting Association the American Institute of Certified Public Accountants, the Financial Executives Institute, the Institute of Internal Auditors and the National Association of Accountants. Often referred to as the Treadway Commission after its chairman, former SEC Commissioner James C. Treadway, Jr., the commission sought to identify the reasons for fraudulent financial reporting and to make recommendations to improve reporting quality.

The commission issued its report in 1987 and addressed several issues pertaining to internal controls, including the importance of the control environment, codes of conduct, engaged audit committees and an active and objective internal audit function. The report called for management reports on the effectiveness of internal control, and called for the sponsoring organizations to work together to integrate the various internal control concepts and definitions.

Subsequently, the Committee of Sponsoring Organizations published the results of an extensive study of internal control practices and a review of the accounting literature on the subject. The report, *Internal Control—Integrated Framework*, was released in 1992. The framework is intended to: (1) include widely-accepted criteria designed to facilitate the establishment of internal control; (2) define the role and responsibility of management; and (3) provide for consistent and recognized means to monitor, evaluate and report on the effectiveness of the control structure. In 1994, the framework was modified to address additional control issues pertaining to the safeguarding of assets, and in 1996, COSO published an additional report on control issues in connection with derivatives.

According to the COSO report, an initial problem with developing a functional internal control framework is coming up with a workable and accepted definition of the concept, as different individuals and entities approach the idea of internal control from widely varying perspectives. The report stated that "this causes confusion among businesspeople, legislators, regulators and others and the resulting miscommunication and different expectations cause problems within an enterprise." According to COSO, "problems are compounded when the term, if not clearly defined, is written into law, regulation or rule."

The report defined internal control as "a process, affected by an entity's board of directors, management and other personnel, designed to provide reasonable assurance regarding the achievement of defined objectives." These objectives are: (1) effectiveness and efficiency of operations, which involves the entity's basic business objectives, performance and profitability goals and the safeguarding of resources; (2) reliability of financial reporting; and (3) compliance with applicable laws and regulations.

The COSO framework is a process-oriented approach rather than any particular set of rules and requirements. This definition extends beyond the traditional concept of internal control as primarily an aspect of financial accounting practices and procedures. Under this structure, internal control is an on-going and integral component of operations, emphasizing the role of people in the organization and establishing that all employees are participants with particular responsibilities in the control structure.

Emphasis is also placed on the identification and management of various forms of risks to which the entity may be exposed. According to COSO, the framework is intended to provide reasonable, rather than absolute or unconditional assurances.

The COSO report definition of internal control is broader than that adopted by the SEC in its June 2003 rulemaking. The SEC definition is limited to internal control in the financial reporting context. As adopted by the SEC, internal control is a process designed to provide reasonable assurance regarding the reliability of financial reporting and the preparation of financial statements for external purposes. This concept of internal control does not include the COSO provisions concerning operational aspects, such as performance and profitability goals and safeguarding of resources. The SEC definition also does not include controls intended to foster compliance with those laws and regulations to which the entity is subject. While the rule does not specifically address legal compliance, the SEC definition would, however, include within its limits the applicable laws and regulations pertaining to financial statement preparation.

The SEC stated that such a limited definition was appropriate in light of Section 404's focus on financial reporting and noted that many commenters were concerned about the compliance costs associated even with a more restrictive definition. Additionally, the Commission noted that independent accountants traditionally have not been responsible for reviewing and testing, or attesting to an assessment by management of, internal controls that are outside the boundary of financial reporting.

Under the COSO framework and SEC rules, management is charged with evaluating the effectiveness of internal control. This is a subjective judgment based on a review of the extent that the control elements described below are present and how well they are functioning. Management, including the CEO and CFO, must perform the evaluation, and cannot delegate this task to the company's outside auditors. Both the design and the operating efficiency of the internal structure must be analyzed.

¶ 404   COSO Framework

The COSO framework consists of five interrelated elements. These framework components are: (1) the control environment, (2) risk assessment, (3) control activities, (4) information and communication, and (5) monitoring. Several aspects of the COSO framework may not appear to be directly relevant to Sarbanes-Oxley and SEC practice because they deal with the operational and legal compliance aspects of the COSO internal control definition that are not within the literal scope of the SEC definition. However, companies should be familiar with these elements, as the COSO framework is an integrated one with significant overlap between the elements.

As the PCAOB noted in the release adopting the audit standard concerning internal control, company-level controls across all elements described in the COSO report "might have a pervasive effect on the achievement of many overall objectives of the control criteria." COSO concepts designed to foster operational efficiency may also be viewed generally as sound practices that can facilitate the prevention and detection of fraud.

¶ 405   Control Environment

The control environment may fairly be described as the "conscience" of the organization. The concept refers to the business environment in which individuals with differing responsibilities conduct the company's business and comply with their control obligations. According to the COSO framework, the control environment factors include: (1) the integrity, ethical values and competence of the entity's people; (2) management's philosophy, operating style and organizational structures; and (3) the role of the board of directors.

Although the control environment may be, as described by COSO, the "foundation" for all other components of internal control, it may also be, with so many subjective factors, the most difficult to define and evaluate. Unlike the internal control systems that many companies currently have in place and with which auditors are familiar, the control environment is not transactionally based. It will not be sufficient for management and auditors to merely review specific actions, as the substance of the corporate environment rather than simply the performance of specified procedures must be determined. A "checklist" review of the control environment is not an adequate approach to evaluating the effectiveness of this vital component.

Companies will need to have in place both "hard" controls and so-called "soft" controls. Hard controls would include elements such as clearly-defined organizational structures, specifically identified and authorized delegations of authority and reporting responsibilities, as well as ample written documentation of hiring, training and other human resource policies. The areas covered by soft controls involve matters that are more difficult to identify and analyze, such as controls dealing with ethics, attitudes, operating styles, effective communications, competence and professionalism.

"Tone at the Top"

A key component of the control environment is the so-called "tone at the top." In its 1987 report, the Treadway Commission emphasized the importance of establishing an appropriate tone at the top and of improving the overall control environment. The subsequent study of financial fraud sponsored by COSO in 1998 reported that this remained a key area in need of improvement. In most of the companies involved in financial fraud, the study found that senior executives were frequently involved in alleged fraudulent conduct. Audit committees were often disengaged and boards of directors were dominated by insiders and outside directors with close ties to the company.

The SEC has also long stressed the importance of the control environment. In a 1981 policy statement issued in connection with the enactment of the Foreign Corrupt Practices Act (see Release No. 34-17500), the SEC stated that the appropriate level of internal control "is not satisfied if a company's leadership, while making nominal gestures of compliance, abdicates its responsibilities to foster integrity among those who operate the system." The SEC concluded that "regardless of how technically sound an issuers controls are, or how impressive they appear on paper, it is unlikely that control objectives will be met in the absence of a supportive environment." "In the last analysis," stated the SEC, "the key to an adequate control environment is an approach on the part of the board and top management which makes clear what is expected, and that conformity to these expectations will be rewarded while breaches will be punished."

The COSO report assigns ultimate responsibility for setting the tone at the top to the CEO. According to COSO, it is the responsibility of the CEO to "assume ownership" of the system. The CEOs of large companies are expected to lead by example and to demonstrate high levels of integrity and ethical values. The heads of smaller companies are also expected to provide positive ethical leadership, but these officers may often have a more active, hands-on approach.

Management is expected to both define expected standards of conduct and to effectively communicate these standards down throughout the structure of the entity. Company management is charged with providing sufficient guidance for proper behavior, removing temptations to unethical behavior and providing effective and responsive discipline when appropriate. Active, engaged directors also contribute to a positive control environment, stated the COSO report. Directors are urged to be objective, capable and inquisitive in the performance of their duties.

Other Control Environment Aspects

The COSO framework calls for a commitment on the part of management to competence. In a positive control environment as defined by COSO, management must define essential competencies and develop training and evaluation procedures to foster these competencies. Employees are expected to demonstrate a level of competence with regard to both their job performance and their roles in the internal control process.

The operating style and general philosophy of management is also an element of the control environment. Included within the concept of management philosophy toward performance goals and performance-based compensation. Of concern here, noted COSO, is that unrealistic expectations or excessive performance-based compensation could lead to misconduct. The responsiveness of management to adverse news and the existence of regular channels for reporting misconduct are also relevant to determining management's philosophy and operating style. The degree of risk the company is willing to take is also a key component of the control environment.

A company's organizational structure is also a significant component of the environmental aspect. The organizational structure provides the framework for planning, directing and controlling operations as necessary to meet the objectives of the company. Areas of authority and reporting channels should be clearly defined in writing and made readily available throughout the company.

Human resource policies also fall within this area. Management is charged with developing and implementing appropriate policies for all human capital areas. These include such areas as hiring, training and orientation, regular evaluations and employee assistance, promotions and compensation and discipline.

COSO formulated some basic questions for companies to consider in assessing their control environment. According to COSO, companies should ask whether:

- board members and senior executives set a regular example of high integrity and ethical behavior;

- there is a written code of conduct for employees;

- conduct expectations are reinforced by training, effective communications and requirements for periodic written statements of compliance from key employees;

- performance and incentive compensation targets areas are reasonable and realistic and do not create undue pressure on achievement of short-term results;

- all personnel at all levels know and understand that fraudulent financial reporting at any level and in any form will not be tolerated;

¶ 405

- ethics are woven into criteria that are used to evaluate individual and business unit performance;

- management reacts appropriately after receiving negative news from subordinates and business units;

- a documented and well-publicized process exists to resolve close ethical calls; and

- business risks are identified and candidly discussed with the board of directors.

Banking Industry Experience

Companies may also find useful guidance by looking at the experience of the banking industry. A similar internal control requirement for depository institutions was enacted in 1991 in amendments to Section 36 of the Federal Deposit Insurance Act. This provision requires financial institutions to have an adequate system of internal control established and evaluated according to some generally accepted framework. Most institutions have selected the COSO framework.

The Federal Deposit Insurance Corporation adopted rules in 1993 to implement. Under these rules, an insured depository institution with total assets of $500 million or more must prepare an annual management report that contains: (1) a statement of management's responsibilities for preparing the institutions annual financial statements, for establishing and maintaining an adequate internal control structure and procedures for financial reporting, and for complying with designated laws and regulations relating to safety and soundness; and (2) management's assessment of the effectiveness of the institutions internal control structure and procedures for financial reporting as of the end of the fiscal year and the institutions compliance with the designated laws and regulations during the fiscal year. The institutions independent public accountant must also examine and attest to management's assertions concerning the effectiveness of the institutions internal controls over financial reporting.

The Office of the Comptroller of the Currency has issued a handbook on internal control that provides guidance for companies now subject to internal control requirements to use when evaluating the control environment. (See Internal Control—Comptroller's Handbook (January 2001).) As described above as required by the COSO framework, the OCC suggests that entities evaluate the integrity, ethics and competence of personnel, the organizational structure of the company, management's philosophy and operating style and personnel policies and practices. In addition, any external influences affecting operations and practices should be considered.

The OCC also emphasized the importance of an active and engaged board of directors. In evaluating the control environment, OCC advised that the examiner should determine the level of attention and direction provided by the board of directors and its committees, especially the audit or risk managementCommittees and whether the board periodically reviews policies and procedures to ensure that proper risk assessment and control processes have been instituted.

The examination should also determine whether there is an audit or other control system in place to periodically test and monitor compliance with internal control policies and procedures and to report instances of noncompliance to the board, if the board reviews the qualifications and independence of internal and external auditors and if auditors report their findings directly to the board or its audit committee.

The comptroller's handbook also advised that a review of the control environment should determine if the board takes appropriate follow-up action when instances of non-compliance are reported. Board procedures, including the extent of access by the board and its representatives to all necessary records and information and the board's decision-making process should also be reviewed. The handbook stated that the examination should determine if board decisions are made collectively or whether dominant individuals control those decisions.

The review should determine if the board or management adequately communicates policies regarding the importance of internal control and appropriate conduct to all employees. It should also be determined if codes of conduct or ethics policies exist and whether audit or other control systems exist to periodically test for compliance with codes of conduct or ethics policies. Finally, the handbook advised that the review should determine if audit or other control system personnel routinely review policies and training regarding ethics or codes of conduct.

In its discussion of the audit standard concerning internal control, the PCAOB recognized the pervasive effect of the control environment on the reliability of financial reporting. The board described the importance of company-level controls within the control environment, including tone at the top, the assignment of authority and responsibility, consistent policies and procedures and company-wide programs such as codes of conduct and fraud prevention that apply to all locations and business units. The board noted that the auditors' preliminary judgment about the effectiveness of the control environment "often influences the nature, timing and the extent of the necessary tests for determining operating effectiveness." "Weaknesses in the control environment should cause the auditor to alter the nature, timing, or extent of tests of operating effectiveness that otherwise should have been performed in the absence of the weaknesses," concluded the board.

¶ 406   Risk Assessment

Risk assessment requires the identification, assessment and analysis of relevant risks that the entity does or might face. Companies will be required, after identifying the relevant risks, to determine if sufficient controls apply to particular risk areas and to correct any inadequate controls.

Under COSO, risk assessment is defined as the process used by management to determine how it will address these risks that may pose a threat to the achievement of defined objectives. Risk assessment allows companies to effectively allocate resources to most effectively meet these challenges to the achievement of the company's business goals. Accordingly, a vital initial step in this process is the definition of clear and consistent company objectives.

This element of risk management demonstrates the inter-related nature of the components of the COSO framework. The philosophy of management toward risk and the degree of risk the entity is willing to entertain is an ingredient of management philosophy, as described in connection with the control environment. management's orientation with regard to the degree of acceptable risk is also an essential component of the risk assessment process.

In addition, the risk assessment aspect reflects the defined objectives of the COSO framework for internal control. Entities must define their operational, reporting and compliance objectives and evaluate the associated risks in each context. A positive control structure will specifically define these objectives throughout all levels of the entity.

The COSO framework recognizes the simple business reality that no entity can identify or insulate itself from all potential risks. Therefore, the assessment process involves a balancing of the likelihood and impact of the identified risks.

Risk identification under the COSO framework may involve several different activities. Qualitative and quantitative ranking activities, management conferences, forecasting and strategic planning and reviews of audits and other studies may be appropriate. A thorough analysis of the possible effect of these identified risks is then required. Management must analyze the risks to determine the likelihood of occurrence and what actions are necessary to manage the risk. This is not a "one size fits all" review, as the size and business activity of the organization will have a significant impact on the nature and scope of possible risks and the nature of the activities needed to manage these risks.

One of the keys to risk assessment is the changing business environment. Shifts in the general condition of the economy, industry conditions and the regulatory and legislative environment may profoundly affect the nature of the risks faced by an entity. As stated by COSO in its definition, internal control is an ongoing process, and a shifting environment requires constant scrutiny in this area.

COSO advised that companies should determine if relevant and reliable internal and external information is identified, compiled and communicated to those positioned to act in a timely fashion. The company must determine if all risks are identified, analyzed and mitigated and if controls are in place to assure that management decisions are properly carried out.

In the OCC handbook described above, with regard to risk assessment, the objective is to determine whether the institutions risk assessment system allows the board and management to plan for and respond to existing and emerging risks in the institutions activities. Accordingly, management should determine whether:

- the board and management involve audit personnel or other internal control experts in the risk assessment and risk evaluation process;

- the risk assessment and evaluation process involves sufficient staff members who are competent, knowledgeable and provided with adequate resources;

- the board and management discuss and appropriately evaluate risks and consider control issues during the pre-planning stages for new products and activities;

- audit personnel or other internal control experts are involved when company bank is developing new products and activities; and

- the board and management consider and appropriately address technology issues.

With regard to the auditors' review of controls concerning risk assessment, the PCAOB stated that the auditor should evaluate whether management has identified the risks of material misstatement in the company's significant accounts and disclosures and related assertions of the financial statements and has implemented controls to prevent or detect errors or fraud that could result in material misstatements. As an example, the board noted that the risk assessment process should address how management considers the possibility of unrecorded transactions or identifies and analyzes significant estimates recorded in the financial statements. Risks relevant to reliable financial reporting also relate to specific events or transactions, stated the PCAOB.

¶ 407   Control Activities

These are defined under the COSO framework as the procedures and policies adopted by management to facilitate the execution of management directives. The control activity aspect focuses on the prevention, detection and correction of improper conduct. They help ensure that necessary actions are taken to address risks to achievement of the entity's objectives. Control activities occur throughout the organization, at all levels and in all functions. These activities include a range of activities as diverse as approvals and authorizations for transactions and activities, verifications, reconciliations, reviews of operating performance, security of assets and segregation of duties.

Appropriate recordkeeping for these tasks is also a key component of effective control functions. The policies and procedures for control activities should be set forth in written documentation, but the creation of such documentation is in itself not sufficient. It is essential under the COSO framework that personnel at all levels be familiar with, understand and conscientiously follow all such procedures.

Accountability is a key element of effective control activities. While it may appear as described above that many of the control activities described in the COSO report do not directly impact financial reporting in terms of SEC compliance, the controls relating to operational matters such as top level and functional level reviews of actual performance, controls over information processing, proper execution and accurate and timely recording of transactions and events and appropriate documentation of transactions may have a significant impact on the reliability of the company's financial reporting.

According to the OCC handbook, the objective of an assessment of the effectiveness of control activities is to determine whether the board and senior management have established effective control activities in all lines of business. The assessment must review whether policies and procedures exist to ensure that decisions are made with appropriate approvals and authorizations for transactions and activities and whether processes exist to ensure that the performance and integrity of each function are independently checked and verified using an appropriate sample of transactions.

The OCC recommends that companies should also have in place safeguards for access to and use of sensitive assets and records, and the assessment should determine if reporting lines within a business or functional area provide sufficient independence of the control function.

The assessment should also include a review of whether: (1) separation of duties are properly emphasized in the organizational structure; (2) systems are in place to ensure that personnel abide by separation of duty requirements; (3) there is an internal review of employee accounts and expense reports; (4) personnel are accountable for the actions they take and the responsibilities and authorities given to them; and (5) operating practices conflict with established areas of responsibility and control.

The examination of the company's control activities should include interviews with line and management personnel, reviews of policies delineating responsibilities and reconciliations and transaction origination. Internal audit work papers and external audit reports should also be examined.

The review should also determine whether internal audit or other control review functions are sufficiently independent. The OCC advised that such an examination should consider:

● where, to whom and at what level the internal audit function reports administratively within the organization;

● whether practices conform to established standards;

● whether management unduly influences the timeliness of risk analysis and control processes; and

● whether the board and senior management has established adequate procedures for ensuring compliance with applicable laws and regulations.

The examination should also determine the frequency of testing and reporting for compliance with laws and regulations by reviewing: (1) audit schedules, scopes and reports; (2) minutes of senior management and board committees; and (3) the payment of any fines or liabilities arising from litigation against the institution or its employees. It is also important, stated the OCC, to determine whether appropriate attention and follow-up are given to violations of laws and regulations. The significance and frequency of the violations and the willingness and ability to prevent reoccurrence should be considered.

According to the PCAOB, the auditors' understanding of control activities relates to the controls that management has implemented to prevent or detect errors or fraud that could result in material misstatement in the accounts and disclosures and related assertions of the financial statements. The board stated that for the purposes of evaluating the effectiveness of internal control over financial reporting, the auditors' understanding of control activities encompasses a broader range of accounts and disclosures than what is normally obtained for the financial statement audit.

¶ 408   Information and Communication

According to COSO, pertinent information must be identified, captured and communicated in a form and timeframe that enable people to carry out their responsibilities. Communication as used by COSO refers not only to reports containing operational, financial and compliance-related information but also to the flow of information in all directions throughout the company. "All personnel must receive a clear message from top management that control responsibilities must be taken seriously," stated the COSO report. All personnel should understand their particular role and duties in the internal control system. The report also stressed the importance of having a means of communicating significant information "upstream" and with having effective communication with external parties, such as customers, suppliers, regulators and shareholders.

According to the OCC handbook, several steps are necessary to determine if internal controls and information systems are appropriate. To assess the adequacy of the company's accounting systems, a review should consider whether accounting systems properly identify, assemble, analyze, classify, record and report transactions in accordance with GAAP, and whether the systems account for the assets and liabilities involved in transactions.

With regard to an assessment of the adequacy of information systems, the review should consider: (1) the type and extent of reports generated for operational, financial, managerial, and compliance-related activities; and (2) whether reports are sufficient to properly run and control the company.

An assessment of the adequacy of communication systems should include a determination of whether significant information is imparted throughout the institution from the top down and from the bottom up in the organizational chain, ensuring that all personnel understand their roles in the control system and how their activities relate to others. The accountability of individuals for the activities they conduct should also be reviewed. The review should also determine if information is imparted to external parties such as regulators, shareholders and customers.

According to the PCAOB, the auditors' understanding of management's information and communication involves understanding the same systems and processes that he or she addresses in an audit of financial statements. In addition, the board asserted that this understanding includes a greater emphasis on comprehending the safeguarding controls and the processes for authorization of transactions and the maintenance of records, as well as the period-end financial reporting process.

¶ 409   Monitoring

The COSO framework stresses the importance of monitoring the internal control system. As defined by COSO, monitoring is "a process that assesses the quality of the systems performance over time." Monitoring consists of both ongoing oversight activities and separate evaluations.

Ongoing monitoring occurs in the course of operations, stated COSO. The process involves regular management and supervisory activities, as well as other actions that other personnel take in the course of their duties. COSO stated that the scope and frequency of separate evaluations will depend primarily on an assessment of risks and the effectiveness of ongoing monitoring procedures.

The OCC handbook advised that a review of the monitoring function should determine whether senior management and the board provides appropriate oversight and attention to internal controls, control reviews and audit findings. It is important to determine whether senior management and the board or appropriate board committees have reviewed actions taken by management to deal with material control weaknesses and verified that those actions are objective and adequate.

To do so, the review should consider minutes of appropriate meetings, audit or other control review reports and follow-up reports and the frequency and comprehensiveness of reports to the board or board committees and senior management. The review should also determine the adequacy of the review of audit and other control functions by the audit or other appropriate board committee.

It is also important to assess the adequacy and independence of the audit or other control review function. The review should consider: (1) results of the review of internal or external audit or other control review working papers; (2) organizational structure and reporting lines; (3) the scope and frequency of audits or reviews for all lines of business; and (4) audit or control review reports, management responses, and follow-up reports.

The PCAOB stated that the auditors' understanding of management's monitoring of controls extends to and includes its monitoring of all controls. This includes control activities that management has identified and designed to prevent or detect material misstatement in the accounts and disclosures and related assertions of the financial statements.

¶ 410   Control Expectations

The COSO framework defined reasonable expectations for internal controls and described what control systems can and cannot do. Internal control can help an entity achieve its performance and profitability targets, prevent loss of resources, ensure reliable financial reporting, and ensure that the enterprise complies with laws and regulations, avoiding damage to its reputation and other consequences. "In sum," stated COSO, "it can help an entity get to where it wants to go, and avoid pitfalls and surprises along the way."

COSO recognized, however, that internal control cannot guarantee the success of an enterprise, ensure effective management, or prevent negative impacts of outside influences, such as shifts in government policy or programs, competitors' actions or economic conditions. The framework also noted that control systems are not infallible and can be circumvented. "Thus, while internal control can help an entity achieve its objectives, it is not a panacea," concluded the report.

CHAPTER 5

AUDITOR ATTESTATION

Introduction . . . . ¶ 501

Overview of Auditing Standard No. 2 . . . . ¶ 502

Management's Responsibilities . . . . ¶ 503

Auditor Independence . . . . ¶ 504

Due Care . . . . ¶ 505

Materiality Considerations . . . . ¶ 506

Fraud Considerations . . . . ¶ 507

Audit Committee's Effectiveness . . . . ¶ 508

¶ 501   Introduction

Sarbanes-Oxley Act Section 404(b) requires every registered public accounting firm that prepares or issues an audit report for a company to attest to, and report on, the assessment of internal controls made by company management. The attestation and report required by Section 404(b) must be made in accordance with standards for attestation engagements issued or adopted by the Public Company Accounting Oversight Board. See Sarbanes-Oxley Act Section 103.

Implementing the statute, SEC rules require independent public auditors to attest to and report on management's assessment of the effectiveness of the company's internal control over financial reporting. Further, although Section 404(b) does not expressly direct it, the SEC rules require a company to file, as part of its annual report, the attestation report of the registered public accounting firm that audited the company's financial statements. The SEC believes it is essential in satisfying the statutory purposes to require a company to file both the internal control report and the auditor's attestation report in the annual report.

Regulation S-X Rule 2-02 permits the auditor to combine the attestation report on management's assessment on internal control with the auditor's report on the financial statements. The SEC staff has advised that, in determining whether to combine the reports, the auditor should take into account any issues that may arise if its audit report on the financial statements is expected to be reissued or incorporated by reference into a filing under the Securities Act. (See FAQ of June 23, 2004, Q. 15.)

Sarbanes-Oxley Act Section 103 directs the Public Company Accounting Oversight Board to adopt auditing standards that would require all registered public accounting firms to present in each audit report or in a separate report:

- the scope of the auditor's testing of the internal control structure and procedures of the issuer;

- the findings of the auditor from such testing;

- the auditor's evaluation of whether such internal control structure and procedures include maintenance of records that in reasonable detail accurately and fairly reflect the transactions and dispositions of the assets of the issuer, provide reasonable assurance that transactions are recorded as necessary to permit preparation of financial statements in accordance with generally accepted accounting principles, and that receipts and expenditures of the issuer are being made only in accordance with authorizations of management and directors of the issuer; and

- a description, at a minimum, of material weaknesses in such internal controls, and of any material noncompliance found on the basis of such testing.

Under Sarbanes-Oxley, the PCAOB has become the body that sets auditing and attestation standards for registered public accounting firms to use in the preparation and issuance of audit reports on the financial statements of issuers. Thus, the PCAOB sets the standards for the accounting firms' attestations to, and reports on, management's assessment regarding its internal control over financial reporting.

¶ 502   Overview of Auditing Standard No. 2

The Public Company Accounting Oversight Board adopted Auditing Standard No. 2, An Audit of Internal Control Over Financial Reporting Performed in Conjunction With an Audit of Financial Statements, in March 2004. Standard No. 2 is the standard on attestation engagements referred to in Sarbanes-Oxley Act Section 404(b).

In preparing the standard, the Board was guided by a number of broad considerations that have effect throughout the provision. These considerations include the following:

- that attestation is insufficient to describe the process of assessing management's report on internal controls;

- that an audit of internal control over financial reporting must be integrated with an audit of the company's financial statements; and

● that the costs of the internal control audit be appropriate in consideration of the expected benefits to investors of improved internal control over financial reporting.

The Board has noted that the two terms, "audit of internal control over financial reporting" and "attestation of management's assessment of the effectiveness of internal control over financial reporting," refer to the same professional service. The first refers to the process, and the second refers to the result of that process.

Costs

The Board has been fully sensitive to the costs of Section 404 and Auditing Standard No. 2, particularly on small and medium-sized companies. But the Board does anticipate that most companies of all sizes will experience the highest cost of complying with Section 404 during the first year of implementation.

That said, it is also true that internal control is not one-size-fits-all, and the nature and extent of controls that are necessary depend, to a great extent, on the size and complexity of the company. Large, complex, multi-national companies, for example, are likely to need extensive and sophisticated internal control systems.

In smaller companies, or in companies with less complex operations, the ethical behavior and core values of a senior management group that is directly involved in daily interactions with both internal and external parties might reduce the need for elaborate internal control systems. The Board expects that the auditor will exercise reasonable professional judgment in determining the extent of the audit of internal control and perform only those tests that are necessary to ascertain the effectiveness of the company's internal control.

Using the Work of Others

The Board also was cognizant of audit costs in its consideration of the appropriate extent to which the auditor may use the work of internal auditors and others to support the auditor's opinion on internal control effectiveness.

Auditing Standard No. 2 provides the auditor with significant flexibility in using the relevant work of highly competent and objective personnel, while also requiring them to obtain through their own auditing procedures a meaningful portion of the evidence that supports the auditor's opinion. The Board believes it has achieved an appropriate balance of work between the auditor and others that will ensure a high quality audit of internal control and that have the complementary benefit of encouraging companies to invest in competent and objective internal audit functions.

¶ 502

Audit Process

An audit of internal control over financial reporting is an extensive process involving several steps, including planning the audit, evaluating the process management used to perform the assessment of internal control effectiveness, obtaining an understanding of the internal control, evaluating the effectiveness of both the design and operation of the internal control, and forming an opinion about whether internal control over financial reporting is effective.

The auditor's objective is to express an opinion about whether management's assessment, or conclusion, on the effectiveness of internal control over financial reporting is stated fairly, in all material respects.

To support that opinion, the auditor must obtain evidence about whether internal control over financial reporting is effective. The auditor obtains this evidence in several ways, including evaluating and testing management's assessment process; evaluating and testing work on internal control performed by others, such as internal auditors; and testing the effectiveness of the controls themselves.

¶ 503   Management's Responsibilities

Citing Regulation S-K Item 308, the PCAOB believes that management has certain responsibilities it must fulfill in an audit of the company's internal controls. Specifically, for the auditor to satisfactorily complete an audit of internal control over financial reporting, management must:

● Accept responsibility for the effectiveness of the company's internal control over financial reporting;

● Evaluate the effectiveness of the company's internal control over financial reporting using suitable control criteria;

● Support its evaluation with sufficient evidence, including documentation; and

● Present a written assessment of the effectiveness of the company's internal control over financial reporting as of the end of the company's most recent fiscal year. (Auditing Standard No. 2, Paragraph 20; see Release No. 34-49544 (SEC 2004), FED. SEC. L. REP. ¶ 87,203.)

Auditors concluding that management has not fulfilled the above responsibilities should communicate, in writing, to management and the audit committee that the audit of internal control over financial reporting cannot be satisfactorily completed and that they are required to disclaim an opinion. (Paragraph 21; see Release No. 34-49544, supra.)

In this situation, an auditor could not render either an adverse opinion on management's assessment or an unqualified opinion on internal control over financial reporting because the auditor would be precluded from expressing any opinion. (See FAQ of June 23, 2004, Q. 8.) In addition, to the extent that management has willfully decided not to fulfill these responsibilities, the auditor also may have responsibilities under AU Section 317 and Exchange Act Section 10A.

¶ 504   Auditor Independence

PCAOB Auditing Standard No. 2 explicitly prohibits the auditor from accepting an engagement to provide an audit client with an internal control-related service that has not been specifically pre-approved by the audit committee. (Paragraph 33; see Release No. 34-49544 (SEC 2004), FED. SEC. L. REP. ¶ 87,203.) This stricture means that the audit committee cannot pre-approve internal control-related services as a category, but must approve each service.

This prohibition is in keeping with the auditor independence principles of the Sarbanes-Oxley Act and the SEC rules under which auditors impair their independence if they audit their own work, including any work on designing or implementing an audit client's internal control system. Thus, embodied in the standard are the four key principles undergirding auditor independence:

● Auditors must not act as management or as an employee of the audit client;

● Auditors must not audit their own work;

● Auditors must not serve in a position of being an advocate for their clients; and

● Auditors must not have mutual or conflicting interests with their clients. (See Preliminary Note of Regulation S-X Rule 2-01.)

For example, if auditors were to design or implement controls, that situation would place them in a management role and result in them auditing their own work. But the Board has advised that these requirements do not preclude the auditor from making substantive recommendations as to how management may improve the design or operation of the company's internal controls as a by-product of an audit. (Paragraph 32; see Release No. 34-49544 (SEC 2004), FED. SEC. L. REP. ¶ 87,203.)

The auditor must not accept an engagement to provide internal control-related services to an issuer for which the auditor also audits the financial statements unless that engagement has been specifically pre-approved by the audit committee. (Paragraph 33; see Release No. 34-49544, supra.)

For any internal control services the auditor provides, management must be actively involved and cannot delegate responsibility for these matters to the auditor. Moreover, management's involvement must be substantive and extensive, emphasized the Board. (Paragraph 33; see Release No. 34-49544, supra.)

Note that management's acceptance of responsibility for documentation and testing performed by the auditor does not by itself satisfy the independence requirements.

It is axiomatic, and has been reiterated by the Board, that maintaining independence, in fact and appearance, requires careful attention, when work concerning internal control over financial reporting is performed. Unless the auditor and the audit committee are diligent in evaluating the nature and extent of services provided, the services might violate basic principles of independence and cause an impairment of independence in fact or appearance. (Paragraph 34; see Release No. 34-49544, supra.)

Staff Guidance

The PCAOB staff has pointed out that the pre-approval requirement applies to any internal control-related services, regardless of whether they are classified as audit or non-audit services for proxy disclosure purposes or otherwise. (See FAQ of June 23, 2004.)

The staff reasoned that every proposed engagement by the company's auditor to provide internal control-related services merits specific attention by the audit committee so that the audit committee can determine whether the performance of the services would impair the auditor's independence and whether management's involvement in the services is substantive and extensive.

Furthermore, the staff has indicated that there is no grandfathering for internal control-related engagements pre-approved prior to the effective date of Auditing Standard No. 2 in a manner that would not satisfy the standard's requirements if the provision of services is ongoing after the effective date. (See FAQ of June 23, 2004.)

If the auditor has been engaged to perform internal control-related services that were pre-approved prior to the effective date in a manner that does not satisfy the standard's requirements, and if those services are ongoing after the effective date, the staff advises the auditor to request the audit committee to specifically evaluate the independence implications of the continuation of those services as soon as practicable.

The staff views this type of remedial involvement of the audit committee as being consistent with the emphasis and vigilance that is appropriate for the committee to have regarding approval of internal control-related services.

Tests for Independence

The independent auditor and the audit committee have significant and distinct responsibilities for evaluating whether the auditor's services impair independence in fact or appearance. The standard's test for independence in fact is whether the activities would impede the ability of anyone on the engagement team or in a position to influence the engagement team from exercising objective judgment in the audits of the financial statements or internal control over financial reporting. (Paragraph 35; see Release No. 34-49544 (SEC 2004), FED. SEC. L. REP. ¶ 87,203.)

The test for independence in appearance is whether a reasonable investor, knowing all relevant facts and circumstances, would perceive an auditor as having interests that could jeopardize the exercise of objective and impartial judgments on all issues encompassed within the auditor's engagement. (Paragraph 35; see Release No. 34-49544, supra.)

¶ 505   Due Care

The auditor must exercise due professional care in an audit of internal control over financial reporting. One important tenet of due professional care is exercising professional skepticism.

In an audit of internal controls, exercising professional skepticism involves essentially the same considerations as in an audit of financial statements, that is, it includes a critical assessment of the work that management has performed in evaluating and testing controls. (Auditing Standard No. 2, Paragraph 36; see Release No. 34-49544 (SEC 2004), FED. SEC. L. REP. ¶ 87,203.)

¶ 506   Materiality Considerations

The standard directs the auditor to apply the concept of materiality in an audit of internal control over financial reporting at both the financial-statement level and at the individual account-balance level. (Auditing Standard No. 2, Paragraph 22; see Release No. 34-49544 (SEC 2004), FED. SEC. L. REP. ¶ 87,203.)

The auditor uses materiality at the financial-statement level inevaluating whether a deficiency, or combination of deficiencies, in controls is a significant deficiency or a material weakness. Materiality at both the financial-statement level and the individual account-balance level is relevant to planning the audit and designing procedures. Materiality at the account-balance level is necessarily lower than materiality at the financial-statement level.

The same conceptual definition of materiality that applies to financial reporting applies to information on internal control over financial reporting, including the relevance of both quantitative and qualitative considerations.

The quantitative considerations are essentially the same as in an audit of financial statements and relate to whether misstatements that would not be prevented or detected by internal control over financial reporting, individually or collectively, have a quantitatively material effect on the financial statements.

The qualitative considerations apply to evaluating materiality with respect to the financial statements and to additional factors that relate to the perceived needs of reasonable persons who will rely on the information.

In this context, the Board reminds auditors that persons who rely on the information concerning internal control over financial reporting include investors, creditors, the board of directors and audit committee, and regulators in specialized industries, such as banking or insurance. (Paragraph 6; see Release No. 34-49544, supra.)

The auditor should be aware that external users of financial statements are interested in information on internal controls because it enhances the quality of financial reporting and increases their confidence in financial information, including financial information issued between annual reports, such as quarterly information.

Information on internal control over financial reporting is also intended to provide an early warning to those inside and outside the company who are in a position to insist on improvements in internal control over financial reporting, such as the audit committee and regulators in specialized industries.

¶ 507   Fraud Considerations

The Board advises the auditor to evaluate all controls specifically intended to address the risks of fraud that have at least a reasonably possible likelihood of having a material effect on the company's financial statements. These controls may be a part of any of the five components of internal control over financial reporting: control environment, control activities, risk assessment, communication, and monitoring. (Auditing Standard No. 2, Paragraph 24; see Release No. 34-49544 (SEC 2004), FED. SEC. L. REP. ¶ 87,203.)

Controls related to the prevention and detection of fraud often have a pervasive effect on the risk of fraud. Such controls include, but are not limited to:

● Controls restraining misappropriation of company assets that could result in a material misstatement of the financials;

● Company's risk assessment processes;

● Code of ethics provisions, especially those related to conflicts of interest, related party transactions, illegal acts, and the monitoring of the code by management and the audit committee;

● Adequacy of the internal audit activity and whether the internal audit function reports directly to the audit committee, as well as the extent of the committee's involvement and interaction with internal audit; and

● Adequacy of the company's procedures for handling complaints and for accepting confidential submissions of concerns about questionable accounting or auditing matters.

In addition, the Board reminds auditors that part of management's responsibility when designing a company's internal controls is to design and implement programs and controls to prevent and detect fraud. Management, along with those who have responsibility for oversight of the financial reporting process (such as the audit committee), should set the proper tone; create and maintain a culture of honesty and high ethical standards; and establish appropriate controls to prevent, deter, and detect fraud. (Paragraph 25; see Release No. 34-49544, supra.)

Finally, in an audit of internal control over financial reporting, the auditor's evaluation of controls is interrelated with the auditor's evaluation of controls in a financial statement audit, as required by AU Section 316.

Controls identified and evaluated by the auditor during the audit of internal controls often also address or mitigate fraud risks, which the auditor must consider in a financial statement audit. If the auditor identifies deficiencies in controls designed to prevent and detect fraud during the audit of internal control over financial reporting, the Board advises the auditor to alter the nature, timing, or extent of procedures to be performed during the financial statement audit to be responsive to such deficiencies. (Paragraph 26; see Release No. 34-49544, supra.)

¶ 508   Audit Committee's Effectiveness

The company's audit committee plays an important role within the control environment and monitoring components of internal control over financial reporting. Within the control environment, the existence of an effective audit committee helps to set a positive tone at the top. Within the monitoring component, an effective audit committee challenges the company's activities in the financial arena.

One of the more notable and controversial aspects of Auditing Standard No. 2 provides that ineffective oversight by the audit committee of the company's external financial reporting and internal controls should be regarded as at least a significant deficiency and is a strong indicator that a material weakness in internal control over financial reporting exists. (Paragraph 59; see Release No. 34-49544 (SEC 2004), FED. SEC. L. REP. ¶ 87,203.)

Board members defended the inclusion of this provision in the standard by emphasizing that the Board could not ignore the key role that audit committees play in the integrity of internal controls. In addition, the Board believes that this is an area where auditors should have a lot to contribute. The major auditing firms deal with hundreds of audit committees, Board Member Daniel Goelzer reasoned, and thus have an ability few others share to compare and contrast performance and to develop expertise concerning best practices. (See remarks at the 22nd Annual Institute on Federal Securities, February 11, 2004.)

Thus, the Board included this provision in the standard for two reasons. (Paragraph E62; see Release No. 34-49544, supra.) First, because of the significant role that the audit committee has in the control environment and monitoring components of internal control over financial reporting, an ineffective audit committee is a gravely serious control weakness that is strongly indicative of a material weakness. Second, highlighting the adverse consequences of an ineffective audit committee would, perhaps, further encourage weak audit committees to improve.

Since the company's board of directors is responsible for evaluating the performance and effectiveness of the audit committee, the standard does not suggest that the auditor is responsible for performing a distinct evaluation of the audit committee. Rather, the Board has consistently emphasized that the auditor's evaluation of the audit committee is not a separate evaluation but, rather, should be made as part of the auditor's evaluation of the control environment and monitoring components of internal control over financial reporting. (Paragraph E66; see Release No. 34-49544, supra.)

Because of the role of the audit committee within the control environment and monitoring components of internal control over financial reporting, the auditor should assess the effectiveness of the audit committee as part of understanding and evaluating those components. (Paragraph 56; see Release No. 34-49544, supra.) The Board recognizes that the aspects of the audit committee's effectiveness that are important may vary considerably with the circumstances.

The auditor focuses on factors related to the effectiveness of the audit committee's oversight of the company's external financial reporting and internal control over financial reporting, such as the independence of the audit committee members from management and the clarity with which the audit committee's responsibilities are articulated (for example, in the audit committee's charter) and how well the audit committee and management understand those responsibilities. (Paragraph 57; see Release No. 34-49544, supra.)

The auditor might also consider the audit committee's involvement and interaction with the independent auditor and with internal auditors, as well as interaction with key members of financial management, including the chief financial officer and chief accounting officer. (Paragraph E69.)

The auditor might also evaluate whether the right questions are raised and pursued with management and the auditor, including questions that indicate an understanding of the critical accounting policies and judgmental accounting estimates, and the responsiveness to issues raised by the auditor. (Paragraph 58.)

On the other hand, factors such as compliance with listing standards and sections of the Sarbanes-Oxley Act should not be evaluated since, in addition to being outside the auditor's expertise, they are not significant to the type of evaluation the auditor is expected to make of the audit committee. (Paragraph E68.)

An auditor who determines that the audit committee's oversight is ineffective should communicate that finding to the full board of directors. This communication should occur regardless of whether the auditor concludes that the condition represents a significant deficiency or a material weakness, and the communication should take place in addition to the normal communication requirements that attach to those deficiencies. (Paragraph E69.)

CHAPTER 6

CONTROL DEFICIENCY AND MATERIAL WEAKNESS

Control Deficiency . . . . ¶ 601
Significant Deficiency . . . . ¶ 602
Material Weakness . . . . ¶ 603

¶ 601   Control Deficiency

A control deficiency exists when the design or operation of a control does not allow management or employees, in the normal course of performing their assigned functions, to prevent or detect misstatements on a timely basis. (Auditing Standard No. 2, Paragraph 8; see Release No. 34-49544 (SEC 2004), FED. SEC. L. REP. ¶ 87,203.)

A deficiency in design exists when a control necessary to meet the control objective is missing or an existing control is not properly designed so that, even if the control operates as designed, the control objective is not always met.

A deficiency in operation exists when a properly designed control does not operate as designed, or when the person performing the control does not possess the necessary authority or qualifications to perform the control effectively.

Compensating Controls

When determining whether a control deficiency exists, the auditor cannot consider compensating controls. (FAQ of June 23, 2004, Q. 12.)

While the PCAOB does allow the effect of compensating controls to be considered in determining whether a control deficiency is a significant deficiency or a material weakness, the staff believes that control deficiencies themselves should be considered individually and in isolation. Thus, the existence of compensating controls does not affect whether a control deficiency exists.

Control Testing Exceptions

The PCAOB staff has indicated that all exceptions to the company's control procedures are not, by definition, control deficiencies. Rather, Auditing Standard No. 2 provides auditors with directions that allow the use of judgment in the circumstances in which they are evaluating whether a control testing exception is a control deficiency. (See FAQ of June 23, 2004, Q. 13.)

For example, a conclusion that an identified control testing exception does not represent a control deficiency is appropriate only if evidence beyond what the auditor had initially planned and beyond inquiry supports that conclusion. (See Paragraph 107; see Release No. 34-49544 (SEC 2004), FED. SEC. L. REP. ¶ 87,203.) In addition, Paragraph 133 includes the example that a control with an observed non-negligible deviation rate is a deficiency.

Both these passages in the standard recognize the inherent limitations in internal control. Effective internal control over financial reporting is a process designed to provide reasonable assurance regarding the reliability of financial reporting. Because effective internal control over financial reporting cannot, and does not, provide absolute assurance of achieving financial reporting objectives, any individual control does not necessarily have to operate perfectly, all the time, to be considered effective.

¶ 602   Significant Deficiency

A significant deficiency is a control deficiency, or combination of control deficiencies, that adversely affects the company's ability to initiate, authorize, record, process, or report external financial data reliably in accordance with generally accepted accounting principles such that there is more than a remote likelihood that a misstatement of the company's annual or interim financial statements that is more than inconsequential will not be prevented or detected.

The term "remote likelihood" as used in the definitions of significant deficiency has the same meaning as the term "remote" as used in FASB Statement No. 5, which defines "remote" as meaning that there is only a slight chance that a future event will confirm the loss or impairment of an asset or the occurrence of a liability.

Therefore, the likelihood of an event is "more than remote" when it is either reasonably possible or probable.

Also, under the standard, a misstatement is inconsequential if a reasonable person would conclude, after considering the possibility of further undetected misstatements, that the misstatement, either individually or when aggregated with other misstatements, would clearly be immaterial to the financial statements. If a reasonable person could not reach such a conclusion regarding a particular misstatement, that misstatement is more than inconsequential.

Staff Guidance

The definition of a significant deficiency is based, in part, on a magnitude of financial statement misstatement that is "more than inconsequential."

According to the staff, a known or likely misstatement aggregated by the auditor as part of the audit of the financial statements is not, by definition, either "more than inconsequential" or determinative of there being a significant deficiency. (See FAQ of June 23, 2004, Q. 11.)TC740 There are several reasons and circumstances why such a likely misstatement aggregated by the auditor might or might not indicate the existence of a significant deficiency.

The definition of inconsequential includes a combination of concepts from both Staff Accounting Bulletin No. 99 on materiality, and AU Section 312. More specifically, the definition is largely based on the discussion of magnitude in SAB No. 99 and on AU Section 312 for its directions regarding both the consideration of misstatements individually and in the aggregate as well as the possibility of undetected misstatements.

The PCAOB consciously avoided a definition of significant deficiency that would be solely dependent on the auditor's judgment since such would be insufficient for the purposes of the Sarbanes-Oxley Act.

This is so because management also needs a definition to determine whether a deficiency is significant, and that definition should be the same as the definition used by the auditor. Thus, Auditing Standard No. 2's definition of significant deficiency is not the same as the auditor's threshold for aggregating likely misstatements in the audit of the financial statements.

The staff recognizes that different auditors exercise their professional judgment in different ways in different circumstances when accumulating likely misstatements as part of the audit of the financial statements. Furthermore, some auditors, as a matter of policy, tend to set their posting threshold for accumulating likely misstatements lower than "inconsequential." For example, they may set their posting threshold for accumulating likely misstatements at 0.25 percent of the company's pre-tax income which would, in most cases, be clearly inconsequential on a quantitative basis.

Because a likely misstatement aggregated by the auditor as part of the audit of the financial statements is not, by definition, "more than inconsequential" or determinative of the existence of a significant deficiency, the staff advises that auditors need not align the amount above which they aggregate misstatements with the amount above which they believe a misstatement to be "more than inconsequential" or determinative of the existence of a significant deficiency.

Further, auditors should not change the types of deficiencies that they determine to be significant deficiencies simply by raising their threshold for accumulating likely misstatements.

These determinations also need to take into consideration qualitative, as well as quantitative, factors. Auditors might still determine that there is a more than remote likelihood that a misstatement larger than the difference on their summary of audit differences might occur and not be prevented or detected. For these reasons, it is possible that a control deficiency associated with a likely misstatement accumulated on their summary of audit differences might indicate the existence of a deficiency, a significant deficiency, or a material weakness.

Compensating Controls

The PCAOB allows the effect of compensating controls to be considered in determining whether a control deficiency is a significant deficiency. Thus, auditors should evaluate the effect of compensating controls when determining whether a control deficiency or combination of deficiencies is a significant deficiency. (See Auditing Standard No. 2, Paragraph 10; see Release No. 34-49544 (SEC 2004), Fed. Sec. L. Rep. ¶ 87,203.)

In order to have a mitigating effect, however, the compensating control should operate at a level of precision that would prevent or detect a misstatement that was more than inconsequential or material, respectively. (See FAQ of June 23, 2004, Q. 14.)

¶ 603   Material Weakness

A material weakness is a significant deficiency, or combination of significant deficiencies, that results in more than a remote likelihood that a material misstatement of the annual or interim financial statements will not be prevented or detected. (Auditing Standard No. 2, Paragraph 10; see Release No. 34-49544 (SEC 2004), Fed. Sec. L. Rep. ¶ 87,203.)

Obviously, the definition of a material weakness relies on the definition of significant deficiency. But this does not mean that a control deficiency, once determined to be only a control deficiency and not also a significant deficiency, can be excluded from the evaluation of whether a significant deficiency or combination of significant deficiencies constitutes a material weakness.

Rather, in the staff's view, if the auditor correctly aggregates control deficiencies when evaluating whether a significant deficiency exists, then all related and salient control deficiencies will also be included in the auditor's evaluation of whether a combination of significant deficiencies represents a material weakness. (See FAQ of June 23, 2004, Q. 15.)

Compensating Controls

The PCAOB allows the effect of compensating controls to be considered in determining whether a control deficiency is a significant deficiency. Thus, auditors should evaluate the effect of compensating controls when determining whether a control deficiency or combination of deficiencies is a material weakness. (See Paragraph 10; see Release No. 34-49544, supra.)

In order to have a mitigating effect, however, the compensating control should operate at a level of precision that would prevent or detect a misstatement that was more than inconsequential or material, respectively. (See FAQ of June 23, 2004, Q. 14.)

CHAPTER 7

PERFORMING AN INTERNAL CONTROL AUDIT

Introduction .... ¶701

Planning the Engagement .... ¶702

Evaluating Management's Assessment Process........ ¶703

Gaining Understanding of Internal Controls .... ¶704

Identifying Processes and Transactions .... ¶705

Performing Walkthroughs .... ¶706

Significant Accounts and Relevant Assertions .... ¶707

Identifying Controls to Test .... ¶708

Testing Effectiveness of Control Design............. ¶709

Testing Operating Effectiveness .... ¶710

Testing in Multiple Locations or Business Units........ ¶711

¶701   Introduction

Generally, in an audit of internal control over financial reporting, the auditor must obtain sufficient competent evidence about the design and operating effectiveness of controls over all relevant financial statement assertions related to all significant accounts and disclosures in the financial statements.

The auditor must plan and perform the audit to obtain reasonable assurance that deficiencies that, individually or in the aggregate, would represent material weaknesses are identified. Thus, the audit is not designed to detect deficiencies in internal controls that, individually or in the aggregate, are less severe than a material weakness.

Because of the potential significance of the information obtained during the audit of the financial statements to the auditor's conclusions about the effectiveness of internal control over financial reporting, the auditor cannot audit internal control over financial reporting without also auditing the financial statements.

Note, however, that the auditor may audit the financial statements without also auditing internal control over financial reporting, for example, in the case of certain initial public offerings by a company.

The auditor must adhere to the general standards in performing an audit of a company's internal control over financial reporting. This involves the following:

● Planning the engagement;

● Evaluating management's assessment process;

● Obtaining an understanding of internal control over financial reporting;

● Testing and evaluating design effectiveness of internal control over financial reporting;

● Testing and evaluating operating effectiveness of internal control over financial reporting; and

● Forming an opinion on the effectiveness of internal control over financial reporting.

Staff Guidance

According to the PCAOB staff, an auditor must test controls directly if management asserts that internal control over financial reporting is ineffective. Further, auditors identifying a material weakness need to complete their testing of controls. (See FAQ of June 23, 2004 Q. 9.)

Auditing Standard No. 2 Paragraph 27 requires the auditor to obtain sufficient competent evidence about the design and operating effectiveness of controls over all relevant financial statement assertions related to all significant accounts and disclosures in the financial statements. (See Release No. 34-49544 (SEC 2004), FED. SEC. L. REP. ¶ 87,203.) That paragraph also requires the auditor to plan and perform the audit to obtain reasonable assurance that all material weaknesses are identified. Thus, the staff reasoned that, to complete an audit of internal control over financial reporting and render an opinion, it is necessary for the auditor to test controls directly, regardless of the company's assessment or the auditor's earlier identification of a material weakness.

¶ 702   Planning the Engagement

The audit of internal control over financial reporting should be properly planned and assistants, if any, must be properly supervised. When planning the audit of internal control over financial reporting, the auditor should evaluate how the following matters will affect the auditor's procedures:

● Knowledge of the company's internal control over financial reporting obtained during other engagements.

● Matters affecting the industry in which the company operates, such as financial reporting practices, economic conditions, laws and regulations, and technological changes.

● Matters relating to the company's business, including its organization, operating characteristics, capital structure, and distribution methods.

● The extent of recent changes, if any, in the company, its operations, or its internal control over financial reporting.

● Management's process for assessing the effectiveness of the company's internal control over financial reporting based on control criteria.

● Preliminary judgments about materiality, risk, and other factors relating to the determination of material weaknesses.

● Control deficiencies previously communicated to the audit committee or management.

● Legal or regulatory matters of which the company is aware.

● The type and extent of available evidence related to the effectiveness of the company's internal control over financial reporting.

● Preliminary judgments about the effectiveness of internal control over financial reporting.

● The number of significant business locations or units, including management's documentation and monitoring of controls over such locations or business units. (Auditing Standard No. 2, Paragraph 39; see Release No. 34-49544 (SEC 2004), Fed. Sec. L. Rep. ¶ 87,203.)

¶ 703   Evaluating Management's Assessment Process

Under the standard's scheme, the natural starting place for the audit of a company's internal control over financial reporting is management's assessment. By evaluating management's assessment, an auditor can have confidence that management has a basis for expressing its conclusion on the effectiveness of internal control.

Such an evaluation also provides information that helps the auditor understand the company's internal control, helps the auditor plan the work necessary to complete the audit, and provides some of the evidence auditors will use to support their opinions.

The work that management performs in connection with its assessment can have a significant effect on the nature, timing, and extent of the work the independent auditor will need to perform. Auditing Standard No. 2 allows the auditor to use, to a reasonable degree, the work performed by others. The more extensive and reliable management's assessment is, the less extensive and costly the auditor's work will need to be.

Also, the more clearly management documents its internal control over financial reporting, the process used to assess the effectiveness of the internal controls, and the results of that process, the easier it will be for the auditor to understand the internal controls, confirm that understanding, evaluate management's assessment, and plan and perform the audit of internal control over financial reporting. This too should translate into reduced professional fees for the audit of internal control over financial reporting.

The auditor should understand how internal control over financial reporting is designed and operates to evaluate and test its effectiveness. The auditor obtains a substantial amount of this understanding when evaluating management's assessment process. More specifically, when obtaining this understanding, the Board wants the auditor to determine whether management has addressed the following eight elements, which are discussed below.

● The first element is determining which controls should be tested, including controls over all relevant assertions related to all significant accounts and disclosures in the financial statements. Generally, such controls include:

—Controls over initiating, authorizing, recording, processing, and reporting significant accounts and disclosures and related assertions embodied in the financial statements.

—Controls over the selection and application of accounting policies that are in conformity with generally accepted accounting principles.

—Antifraud programs and controls.

—Controls, including information technology general controls, on which other controls are dependent.

—Controls over significant nonroutine and nonsystematic transactions, such as accounts involving judgments and estimates.

—Company level controls, including: The control environment and controls over the period-end financial reporting process, including controls over procedures used to enter transaction totals into the general ledger; to initiate, authorize, record, and process journal entries in the general ledger; and to record recurring and nonrecurring adjustments to the financial statements (for example, consolidating adjustments, report combinations, and reclassifications). It should be noted that references to the period-end financial reporting process in this standard refer to the preparation of both annual and quarterly financial statements.

● The second element is evaluating the likelihood that failure of the control could result in a misstatement, the magnitude of such a misstatement, and the degree to which other controls, if effective, achieve the same control objectives.

● The third element is determining the locations or business units to include in the evaluation for a company with multiple locations or business units.

● The fourth element is evaluating the design effectiveness of controls.

● The fifth element is evaluating the operating effectiveness of controls based on procedures sufficient to assess their operating effectiveness. Examples of such procedures include testing of the controls by internal audit, testing of controls by others under the direction of management, using a service organization's reports, inspection of evidence of the application of controls, or testing by means of a self-assessment process, some of which might occur as part of management's ongoing monitoring activities. Inquiry alone is not adequate to complete this evaluation. To evaluate the effectiveness of the company's internal control over financial reporting, management must have evaluated controls over all relevant assertions related to all significant accounts and disclosures.

● The sixth element is determining the deficiencies in internal control over financial reporting that are of such a magnitude and likelihood of occurrence that they constitute significant deficiencies or material weaknesses.

● The seventh element is communicating findings to the auditor and to others, if applicable.

● The eighth element is evaluating whether findings are reasonable and support management's assessment.

According to the Board, as part of the understanding and evaluation of management's process, the auditor should obtain an understanding of the results of procedures performed by others. Others include internal audit and third parties working under the direction of management, including other auditors and accounting professionals engaged to perform procedures as a basis for management's assessment. (Auditing Standard No. 2, Paragraph 41; see Release No. 34-49544 (SEC 2004), FED. SEC. L. REP. ¶ 87,203.)

Inquiry of management and others is the beginning point for obtaining an understanding of internal control over financial reporting, but inquiry alone is not adequate for reaching a conclusion on any aspect of internal controls. The Board has also emphasized that management cannot use the auditor's procedures as part of the basis for its assessment of the effectiveness of the internal controls.

Management's Documentation

When determining whether management's documentation provides reasonable support for its assessment, the auditor should evaluate whether such documentation includes the following:

● The design of controls over all relevant assertions related to all significant accounts and disclosures in the financial statements. The documentation should include the five components of internal control over financial reporting: the control environment, risk assessment, control activities, information and communication, and monitoring.

● Information about how significant transactions are initiated, authorized, recorded, processed and reported;

● Sufficient information about the flow of transactions to identify the points at which material misstatements due to error or fraud could occur;

● Controls designed to prevent or detect fraud, including who performs the controls and the related segregation of duties;

● Controls over the period-end financial reporting process;

● Controls over safeguarding of assets; and

● The results of management's testing and evaluation. (Paragraph 42; see Release No. 34-49544 (SEC 2004), FED. SEC. L. REP. ¶ 87,203.)

Documentation might take many forms, such as paper, electronic files, or other media, and can include a variety of information, including policy manuals, process models, flowcharts, job descriptions, documents, and forms. The Board understands that the form and extent of documentation will vary depending on the size, nature, and complexity of the company. (Paragraph 43; see Release No. 34-49544, supra.)

Documentation of the design of controls over relevant assertions related to significant accounts and disclosures is evidence that controls related to management's assessment of the effectiveness of internal control over financial reporting, including changes to those controls, have been identified, are capable of being communicated to those responsible for their performance, and are capable of being monitored by the company. (Paragraph 44; see Release No. 34-49544, supra.)

Such documentation also provides the foundation for appropriate communication concerning responsibilities for performing controls and for the company's evaluation of and monitoring of the effective operation of controls.

Inadequate documentation of the design of controls over relevant assertions related to significant accounts and disclosures is a deficiency in the company's internal control over financial reporting. As required by other parts of Auditing Standard No. 2, generally Paragraph 138, the auditor should evaluate this documentation deficiency.

The auditor might conclude that the deficiency is only a deficiency, or that the deficiency represents a significant deficiency or a material weakness. In evaluating the deficiency as to its significance, the auditor should determine whether management can demonstrate the monitoring component of internal control over financial reporting.

Inadequate documentation also could cause the auditor to conclude that there is a limitation on the scope of the engagement.

¶ 704   Gaining Understanding of Internal Controls

Under Auditing Standard No. 2, the auditor should obtain an understanding of the design of specific controls by applying procedures that include:

● Making inquiries of appropriate management, supervisory, and staff personnel;

● Inspecting company documents;

● Observing the application of specific controls;

● Tracing transactions through the information system relevant to financial reporting.

The auditor must also obtain an understanding of the design of controls related to each of the five components of internal control over financial reporting. (Paragraph 49; see Release No. 34-49544 (SEC 2004), FED. SEC. L. REP. ¶ 87,203.)

Control Environment

Because of the pervasive effect of the control environment on the reliability of financial reporting, the auditor's preliminary judgment about its effectiveness often influences the nature, timing, and extent of the tests of operating effectiveness considered necessary. Weaknesses in the control environment should cause the auditor to alter the nature, timing, or extent of tests of operating effectiveness that otherwise should have been performed in the absence of the weaknesses.

The SEC staff has advised that, in determining whether to combine the reports, the auditor should take into account any issues that may arise if its audit report on the financial statements is expected to be reissued or incorporated by reference into a filing under the Securities Act. (See FAQ of June 23, 2004, Q. 15.)

Risk Assessment

When obtaining an understanding of the company's risk assessment process, the auditor should evaluate whether management has identified the risks of material misstatement in the significant accounts and disclosures and related assertions of the financial statements and has implemented controls to prevent or detect errors or fraud that could result in material misstatements.

For example, the risk assessment process should address how management considers the possibility of unrecorded transactions or identifies and analyzes significant estimates recorded in the financial statements. Risks relevant to reliable financial reporting also relate to specific events or transactions.

Control Activities

The auditor's understanding of control activities relates to the controls that management has implemented to prevent or detect errors or fraud that could result in material misstatement in the accounts and disclosures and related assertions of the financial statements.

For the purposes of evaluating the effectiveness of internal control over financial reporting, the auditor's understanding of control activities encompasses a broader range of accounts and disclosures than what is normally obtained for the financial statement audit.

Information and Communication

The auditor's understanding of management's information and communication involves understanding the same systems and processes addressed in an audit of financial statements. In addition, this understanding includes a greater emphasis on comprehending the safeguarding controls and the processes for authorization of transactions and the maintenance of records, as well as the period-end financial reporting process.

Monitoring

The auditor's understanding of management's monitoring of controls extends to and includes its monitoring of all controls, including control activities, which management has identified and designed to prevent or detect material misstatement in the accounts and disclosures and related assertions of the financial statements.

General Approach

The auditor should focus on combinations of controls, in addition to specific controls in isolation, in assessing whether the objectives of the control criteria have been achieved. (Paragraph 51; see Release No. 34-49544 (SEC 2004), Fᴇᴅ. Sᴇᴄ. L. Rᴇᴘ. ¶ 87,203.)

¶ 704

The absence or inadequacy of a specific control designed to achieve the objectives of a specific criterion might not be a deficiency if other controls specifically address the same criterion. Further, when one or more controls achieve the objectives of a specific criterion, the auditor might not need to evaluate other controls designed to achieve those same objectives.

The Board recognizes that some controls might have a pervasive effect on the achievement of many overall objectives of the control criteria. (Paragraph 50; see Release No. 34-49544, supra.)

Company-Level Controls

Controls that exist at the company-level are an example of controls that often have a pervasive impact on controls at the process, transaction, or application level. Thus, as a practical consideration, it may be appropriate for the auditor to test and evaluate the design effectiveness of company-level controls first, because the results of that work might affect the way the auditor evaluates the other aspects of internal control over financial reporting. Company-level controls include the following:

● Controls within the control environment, including tone at the top, the assignment of authority and responsibility, consistent policies and procedures, and company-wide programs, such as codes of conduct and fraud prevention, that apply to all locations and business units

● Management's risk assessment process;

● Centralized processing and controls, including shared serviceenvironments;

● Controls to monitor results of operations;

● Controls to monitor other controls, including activities of the internal audit function, the audit committee, and self-assessment programs;

● The period-end financial reporting process; and

● Board-approved policies that address significant business control and risk management practices.

Note that testing company-level controls alone is not sufficient for the purpose of expressing an opinion on the effectiveness of a company's internal control over financial reporting. (Paragraph 54; see Release No. 34-49544, supra.) For example, information technology general controls over program development, program changes, computer operations, and access to programs and data help ensure that specific controls over the processing of transactions are operating effectively.

In contrast, other controls are designed to achieve specific objectives of the control criteria. For example, management generally establishes specific controls, such as accounting for all shipping documents, to ensure that all valid sales are recorded.

Identifying Significant Accounts

The auditor should identify significant accounts and disclosures, first at the financial-statement level and then at the account or disclosure-component level. Determining specific controls to test begins by identifying significant accounts and disclosures within the financial statements. When identifying significant accounts, the auditor should evaluate both quantitative and qualitative factors.

Under the standard, an account is significant if there is more than a remote likelihood that the account could contain misstatements that individually, or when aggregated with others, could have a material effect on the financial statements, considering the risks of both overstatement and understatement. (Paragraph 61; see Release No. 34-49544, supra.)

Other accounts may be significant on a qualitative basis based on the expectations of a reasonable user. For example, investors might be interested in a particular financial statement account even though it is not quantitatively large because it represents an important performance measure.

For purposes of determining significant accounts, the Board wants the assessment as to likelihood to be made without giving any consideration to the effectiveness of internal control over financial reporting. In addition, components of an account balance subject to differing risks or different controls should be considered separately as potential significant accounts. (Paragraph 62; see Release No. 34-49544, supra.) For example, inventory accounts often consist of raw materials (purchasing process), work in process (manufacturing process), finished goods (distribution process), and an allowance for obsolescence.

In some cases, separate components of an account might be a significant account because of the company's organizational structure. For example, for a company that has a number of separate business units, each with different management and accounting processes, the accounts at each separate business unit are considered individually as potential significant accounts.

An account also may be considered significant because of the exposure to unrecognized obligations represented by the account. For example, loss reserves related to a self-insurance program or unrecorded contractual obligations at a construction contracting subsidiary may have historically been insignificant in amount, yet might represent a more than remote likelihood of material misstatement due to the existence of material unrecorded claims.

When deciding whether an account is significant, it is important for the auditor to evaluate both quantitative and qualitative factors, including the:

- Size and composition of the account;

- Volume of activity, complexity, and homogeneity of the individual transactions processed through the account;

- Susceptibility of loss due to errors or fraud;

● Nature of the account (for example, suspense accounts generally warrant greater attention);

● Accounting and reporting complexities associated with the account;

● Exposure to losses represented by the account (for example, loss accruals related to a consolidated construction contracting subsidiary);

● Likelihood of significant contingent liabilities arising from the activities represented by the account;

● Existence of related party transactions in the account; and

● Changes from the prior period in account characteristics (for example, new complexities or subjectivity or new types of transactions).

For example, in a financial statement audit, the auditor might not consider the fixed asset accounts significant when there is a low volume of transactions and when inherent risk is assessed as low, even though the balances are material to the financial statements. Thus, the auditor might decide to perform only substantive procedures on such balances. In an audit of internal control over financial reporting, however, such accounts are significant accounts because of their materiality to the financial statements.

As another example, the auditor of the financial statements of a financial institution might not consider trust accounts significant to the institution's financial statements because such accounts are not included in the institution's balance sheet and the associated fee income generated by trust activities is not material.

However, in determining whether trust accounts are a significant account for purposes of the audit of internal control over financial reporting, the auditor should assess whether the activities of the trust department are significant to the institution's financial reporting, which also would include considering the contingent liabilities that could arise if a trust department failed to fulfill its fiduciary responsibilities.

When assessing the significance of possible contingent liabilities, consideration of the amount of assets under the trust department's control may be useful. For this reason, an auditor who has not considered trust accounts significant accounts for purposes of the financial statement audit might determine that they are significant for purposes of the audit of internal control over financial reporting.

Identifying Relevant Financial Statement Assertions

For each significant account, the auditor should determine the relevance of each of the following five financial statement assertions: existence or occurrence; completeness; valuation or allocation; rights and obligations; and presentation and disclosure.

To identify relevant assertions, the auditor should determine the source of likely potential misstatements in each significant account. In determining whether a particular assertion is relevant to a significant account balance or disclosure, the auditor should evaluate:

- The nature of the assertion;

- The volume of transactions or data related to the assertion; and

- The nature and complexity of the systems, including the use of information technology by which the company processes and controls information supporting the assertion.

The Board defines "relevant assertions" as those with a meaningful bearing on whether the account is fairly stated. (Paragraph 70; see Release No. 34-49544, supra.) For example, valuation may not be relevant to the cash account unless currency translation is involved; however, existence and completeness are always relevant. Similarly, valuation may not be relevant to the gross amount of the accounts receivable balance, but is relevant to the related allowance accounts.

In addition, the auditor might, in some circumstances, focus on the presentation and disclosure assertion separately in connection with the period-end financial reporting process.

Staff Guidance

According to the PCAOB staff, management and the auditor performing an audit of internal controls may base their evaluations on assertions that are different from the five assertions specified in Auditing Standard No. 2. (See FAQ of June 23, 2004, Q. 10.) But the staff reminded that any relevant assertions used would have to have a meaningful bearing on whether the account is fairly stated.

To identify relevant assertions, advised the staff, the auditor should determine the sources of likely potential misstatements in each significant account. Ultimately, management and the auditor should identify and test controls over all relevant assertions for all significant accounts.

To the extent that management or the auditor use assertions different from those in Auditing Standard No. 2, the auditor must determine that he or she had identified and tested controls over all sources of likely potential misstatements in each significant account and over all representations by management that have a meaningful bearing on whether the account is fairly stated.

¶705   Identifying Processes and Transactions

The auditor should identify each significant process over each major class of transactions affecting significant accounts or groups of accounts. Major classes of transactions are those classes of transactions that are significant to the company's financial statements.

> *Example 1:* At a company whose sales may be initiated by customers through personal contact in a retail store or electronically through use of the Internet, these types of sales would be two major classes of transactions within the sales process if they were both significant to the company's financial statements.

> *Example 2:* At a company for which fixed assets is a significant account, recording depreciation expense would be a major class of transactions.

Different types of major classes of transactions have different levels of inherent risk associated with them and require different levels of management supervision and involvement. For this reason, the auditor might further categorize the identified major classes of transactions by transaction type: routine, nonroutine, and estimation.

"Routine transactions" are recurring financial activities reflected in the accounting records in the normal course of business (for example, sales, purchases, cash receipts, cash disbursements, payroll). "Nonroutine transactions" are activities that occur only periodically (for example, taking physical inventory, calculating depreciation expense, adjusting for foreign currencies). A distinguishing feature of nonroutine transactions is that data involved are generally not part of the routine flow of transactions.

"Estimation transactions" are activities that involve management judgments or assumptions in formulating account balances in the absence of a precise means of measurement (for example, determining the allowance for doubtful accounts, establishing warranty reserves, assessing assets for impairment).

Most processes involve a series of tasks such as capturing input data, sorting and merging data, making calculations, updating transactions and master files generating transactions, and summarizing and displaying or reporting data.

The processing procedures relevant for the auditor to understand the flow of transactions generally are those activities required to initiate, authorize, record, process and report transactions. These activities include, for example, initially recording sales orders, preparing shipping documents and invoices, and updating the accounts receivable master file. The relevant processing procedures also include procedures for correcting and reprocessing previously rejected transactions and for correcting erroneous transactions through adjusting journal entries. For each significant process, the auditor should:

● Understand the flow of transactions, including how transactions are initiated, authorized, recorded, processed, and reported.

● Identify the points within the process at which a misstatement, including a misstatement due to fraud, related to each relevant financial statement assertion could arise.

● Identify the controls that management has implemented to address these potential misstatements.

● Identify the controls that management has implemented over the prevention or timely detection of unauthorized acquisition, use, or disposition of the company's assets.

Auditors frequently obtain the understanding and identify the controls described above as part of their performance of walkthroughs.

Understanding Period-End Financial Reporting Process

The period-end financial reporting process includes the following:

● The procedures used to enter transaction totals into the general ledger;

● The procedures used to initiate, authorize, record, and process journal entries in the general ledger;

● Other procedures used to record recurring and nonrecurring adjustments to the annual and quarterly financial statements, such as consolidating adjustments, report combinations, and classifications; and

● Procedures for drafting annual and quarterly financial statements and related disclosures.

The PCAOB staff has explained that the reference to "financial statements and related disclosures" refers to a company's financial statements and notes as presented in accordance with GAAP. The reference does not extend to the preparation of MD&A or other similar financial information presented outside a company's GAAP-basis financial statements and notes. (See FAQ of June 23, 2004.)

As part of understanding and evaluating the period-end financial reporting process, the auditor should evaluate:

● The inputs, procedures performed, and outputs of the processes the company uses to produce its annual and quarterly financial statements;

● The extent of information technology involvement in each period-end financial reporting process element;

● Who participates from management;

● The number of locations involved;

● Types of adjusting entries (for example, standard, nonstandard,eliminating, and consolidating); and

● The nature and extent of the oversight of the process by appropriate parties, including management, the board of directors, and the audit committee.

The period-end financial reporting process is always a significant process because of its importance to financial reporting and to the auditor's opinions on internal control over financial reporting and the financial statements. The auditor's understanding of the company's period-end financial reporting process and how it interrelates with the company's other significant processes assists the auditor in identifying and testing controls that are the most relevant to financial statement risks.

¶ 706   Performing Walkthroughs

The auditor also should be satisfied, however, that the controls actually have been implemented and are operating as designed. Thus, while inquiry of company personnel and a review of management's assessment process provide the auditor with an understanding of how the system of internal control is designed and operates, they are insufficient by themselves. Other procedures are necessary for the auditor to confirm this understanding.

Auditing Standard No. 2 directs the auditor to confirm the understanding by performing procedures that include making inquiries of and observing the personnel who actually perform the controls; reviewing documents that are used in, and that result from, the application of the controls; and comparing supporting documents (for example, sales invoices, contracts, and bills of lading) to the accounting records.

The most effective means of accomplishing this objective is for the auditor to perform walkthroughs of the company's significant processes. To introduce a powerful efficiency, and because of the importance of several other objectives that walkthroughs accomplish, Auditing Standard No. 2 requires the auditor to perform walkthroughs in each annual audit of internal control over financial reporting.

In a walkthrough, the auditor traces a transaction from each major class of transactions from origination, through the company's accounting and information systems and financial report preparation processes, to it being reported in the company's financial statements.

Walkthroughs provide the auditor with audit evidence that supports or refutes an understanding of the process flow of transactions, the design of controls, and whether controls are in operation. Walkthroughs also help to determine if the auditor's understanding is complete and provide information necessary for the auditor to evaluate the effectiveness of the design of the internal control over financial reporting.

Because of the judgment that a walkthrough requires and the significance of the objectives that walkthroughs allow the auditor to achieve, Auditing Standard No. 2 requires auditors to perform the walkthroughs themselves. This means that auditors cannot use the work performed by management or others to satisfy the requirement to perform walkthroughs. To provide additional evidence, however, the auditor may also review walkthroughs that have been performed and documented by others.

The walkthroughs also must be done in each annual audit of internal control over financial reporting. Important objectives of walkthroughs are to confirm that the auditor's understanding of the controls is correct and complete. The Board believes that, without actually walking transactions through the significant processes each year, there is too high a risk that changes to the processes would go undetected by the auditor.

Moreover, because of the significance of the objectives they are intended to achieve, and the judgment necessary to their effective performance, walkthroughs should be performed by appropriately experienced auditors. If inexperienced audit personnel do participate in walkthroughs, the Board emphasized that they should be supervised closely so that the conditions encountered in the walkthroughs are considered appropriately and that the information obtained in the walkthroughs is properly documented.

While performing a walkthrough, the auditor should evaluate the quality of the evidence obtained and perform walkthrough procedures that produce a level of evidence consistent with the objectives. (Auditing Standard No. 2, Paragraph 81; see Release No. 34-49544 (SEC 2004), FED. SEC. L. REP. ¶ 87,203.)

Rather than reviewing copies of documents and making inquiries of a single person at the company, the auditor should follow the process flow of actual transactions using the same documents and information technology that company personnel use and make inquiries of relevant personnel involved in significant aspects of the process or controls.

To corroborate information at various points in the walkthrough, the auditor might ask personnel to describe their understanding of the previous and succeeding processing or control activities and to demonstrate what they do. In addition, inquiries should include follow-up questions that could help identify the abuse of controls or indicators of fraud. Examples of follow-up inquiries include asking personnel:

> ● What they do when they find an error or what they are looking for to determine if there is an error (rather than simply asking them if they perform listed procedures and controls);

> ● What kind of errors they have found; what happened as a result of finding the errors, and how the errors were resolved.

● Whether they have ever been asked to override the process or controls, and if so, to describe the situation, why it occurred, and what happened.

If the person being interviewed has never found an error, the auditor should evaluate whether that situation is due to good preventive controls or whether the individual performing the control lacks the necessary skills.

Finally, during the period under audit, when there have been significant changes in the process flow of transactions, including the supporting computer applications, the auditor should evaluate the nature of the change(s) and the effect on related accounts to determine whether to walk through transactions that were processed both before and after the change. (Paragraph 82; see Release No. 34-49544, supra.)

Unless significant changes in the process flow of transactions, including the supporting computer applications, make it more efficient to prepare new documentation of a walkthrough, auditors may carry their documentation forward each year, after updating it for any changes that havetaken place.

The SEC staff has advised that, in determining whether to combine the reports, the auditor should take into account any issues that may arise if its audit report on the financial statements is expected to be reissued or incorporated by reference into a filing under the Securities Act. (See FAQ of June 23, 2004, Q. 15.)

¶ 707   Significant Accounts and Relevant Assertions

As a part of obtaining an understanding of internal control, the auditor also determines which controls should be tested, either by the auditor, management, or others. Auditing Standard No. 2 requires that the auditor obtain evidence about the operating effectiveness of internal control over financial reporting for all relevant assertions for all significant accounts or disclosures. This requirement relies heavily on two concepts: (1) significant account; and (2) relevant assertion.

Auditing standards implicitly recognize that some accounts are more significant than others. Auditing Standard No. 2 provides additional direction on how to determine significant accounts for purposes of the audit of internal control over financial reporting. In short, the auditor begins by performing a quantitative evaluation of accounts at the financial-statement caption or note-disclosure level. Then the auditor expands the evaluation to include qualitative factors, such as differing risks, company organization structure, and other factors, which would likely result in additional accounts being identified as significant.

Financial statement amounts and disclosures embody financial statement assertions. Obtaining answers to the following questions can help the auditor identify the relevant financial statement assertions for which the company should have controls:

- Does the asset exist?

- Did the transaction occur?

- Has the company included all loans outstanding in its loans payable account?

- Have marketable investments been valued properly?

- Does the company have the rights to the accounts receivable?

- Are the loans payable the proper obligation of the company?

- Are the amounts in the financial statements appropriately presented, and is there adequate disclosure about them?

Identifying relevant assertions is a familiar process for experienced auditors, and because of the importance relevant assertions play in the required extent of testing, Auditing Standard No. 2 provides additional direction.

Similarly, experienced auditors are familiar with identifying significant processes and major classes of transactions. Major classes of transactions are those groupings of transactions that are significant to the company's financial statements. For example, at a company for which sales may be initiated by customers through personal contract in a retail store or electronically using the Internet, these would be two major classes of transactions within the sales process (if they were both significant to the company's financial statements). Because of the importance of significant processes and major classes of transaction in the design of the auditor's procedures, Auditing Standard No. 2 provides additional direction here as well.

¶ 708   Identifying Controls to Test

Auditors should obtain evidence about the effectiveness of controls either by performing tests of controls themselves, or by using the work of others for all relevant assertions related to all significant accounts and disclosures in the financial statements. After identifying significant accounts, relevant assertions, and significant processes, the auditor should evaluate the following to identify the controls to be tested:

- Points at which errors or fraud could occur;

- The nature of the controls implemented by management;

- The significance of each control in achieving the objectives of the control criteria and whether more than one control achieves a particular objective or whether more than one control is necessary to achieve a particular objective; and

● The risk that the controls might not be operating effectively. (Paragraph 83; see Release No. 34-49544 (SEC 2004), Fed. Sec. L. Rep. ¶ 87,203.)

Factors that affect whether the control might not be operating effectively include the following:

● Whether there have been changes in the volume or nature of transactions that might adversely affect control design or operating effectiveness;

● Whether there have been changes in the design of controls;

● The degree to which the control relies on the effectiveness of other controls (for example, the control environment or information technology general controls);

● Whether there have been changes in key personnel who perform the control or monitor its performance;

● Whether the control relies on performance by an individual or isautomated; and

● The complexity of the control.

The auditor should clearly link individual controls with the significant accounts and assertions to which they relate. In addition, the auditor should evaluate whether to test preventive controls, detective controls, or a combination of both for individual relevant assertions related to individual significant accounts. (Auditing Standard No. 2, Paragraph 85; see Release No. 34-49544, supra.)

For instance, when performing tests of preventive and detective controls, the auditor might conclude that a deficient preventive control could be compensated for by an effective detective control and, therefore, not result in a significant deficiency or material weakness.

For example, a monthly reconciliation control procedure, which is a detective control, might detect an out-of-balance situation resulting from an unauthorized transaction being initiated due to an ineffective authorization procedure, which is a preventive control. When determining whether the detective control is effective, the auditor should evaluate whether the detective control is sufficient to achieve the control objective to which the preventive control relates.

Because effective internal control over financial reporting often includes a combination of preventive and detective controls, the auditor ordinarily will test a combination of both.

The auditor should also apply tests of controls to those controls that are important to achieving each control objective. It is neither necessary to test all controls nor is it necessary to test redundant controls (that is, controls that duplicate other controls that achieve the same objective and already have been tested), unless redundancy is itself a control objective, as in the case of certain computer controls. (Paragraph 86; see Release No. 34-49544, supra.)

¶ 709   Testing Effectiveness of Control Design

To be effective, internal controls must be designed properly, and all the controls necessary to provide reasonable assurance about the fairness of a company's financial statements should be in place and performed by appropriately qualified people who have the authority to implement them.

Thus, at some point during the internal control audit, the auditor must determine whether the controls would be effective if they were operated as designed, and whether all the necessary controls are in place. This is known as design effectiveness. The procedures the auditor performs to test and evaluate design effectiveness include:

- inquiries of company personnel,

- observation of internal controls,

- walkthroughs, and

- a specific evaluation of whether the controls are likely to prevent or detect financial statement misstatements if they operate as designed.

Auditing Standard No. 2 adopts these methods of testing and evaluating design effectiveness. The last step is especially important because it calls for auditors to apply professional judgment and knowledge of and experience with internal control over financial reporting to their understanding of the company's controls.

¶ 710   Testing Operating Effectiveness

Auditing Standard No. 2 requires the auditor to obtain evidence about the operating effectiveness of controls related to all relevant financial statement assertions for all significant accounts and disclosures in the financial statements.

For this reason, in addition to being satisfied as to the effectiveness of the design of the internal controls, the auditor performs tests of controls to obtain evidence about the operating effectiveness of the controls. These tests include:

- a mix of inquiries of appropriate company personnel;

- inspection of relevant documentation, such as sales orders and invoices;

- observation of the controls in operation; and

- reperformance of the application of the control.

Auditing Standard No. 2 directs required tests of controls to relevant assertions rather than to significant controls.

To comply with the standard's requirements, the auditor would apply tests to those controls that are important to fairly presenting each relevant assertion in the financial statements. It is neither necessary to test all controls nor is it necessary to test redundant controls, unless redundancy is itself a control objective, as in the case of certain computer controls.

However, the emphasis is better placed on addressing relevant assertions, because those are the points where misstatements could occur, rather than significant controls. This emphasis encourages the auditor to identify and test controls that address the primary areas where misstatements could occur, yet limits the auditor's work to the necessary controls.

Expressing the extent of testing in this manner also resolves the issue of the extent of testing from year to year. Auditing Standard No. 2 states that the auditor should vary testing from year to year, both to introduce unpredictability into the testing and to respond to changes at the company. However, each year's audit must stand on its own. Therefore, the auditor must obtain evidence of the effectiveness of controls for all relevant assertions for all significant accounts and disclosures every year.

At the Board's roundtable, public company representatives and auditors indicated that providing examples of extent-of-testing decisions would be helpful. The proposed auditing standard included several examples, which have been retained in Appendix B of Auditing Standard No. 2.

Timing of Testing

The Act requires management's assessment and the auditor's opinion to address whether internal control was effective as of the end of the company's most recent fiscal year. Thus, performing all of the testing on December 31 is neither practical nor appropriate. To form a basis to express an opinion about whether internal control was effective as of a point in time requires the auditor to obtain evidence that the internal control operated effectively over an appropriate period of time.

Auditing Standard No. 2 recognizes this and allows the auditor to obtain evidence about operating effectiveness at different times throughout the year, provided that the auditor updates those tests or obtains other evidence that the controls still operated effectively at the end of the company's fiscal year.

Staff Guidance

If management implements, late in the year, a new accounting system that significantly affects the processing of transactions for significant accounts, the auditor will have to test controls over the new system even if the majority of the year's transactions were processed on the old system since these are the controls operating as of the date of management's assessment. (See FAQ of June 23, 2004.)

That said, the old system remains relevant to the audit of the financial statements since the auditor should have an understanding of the internal controls, which includes the old system. Additionally, to assess control risk for specific financial statement assertions at less than the maximum, the auditor must obtain evidence that the relevant controls operated effectively during the entire period on which the auditor plans to place reliance on those controls. (See FAQ of June 23, 2004.)

¶ 711   Testing in Multiple Locations or Business Units

Appendix B of Auditing Standard No. 2 provides additional direction to the auditor in determining which controls to test when a company has multiple locations or business units. In these circumstances, the auditor should determine significant accounts and their relevant assertions, significant processes, and major classes of transactions based on those that are relevant and significant to the consolidated financial statements. Having made those determinations in relation to the consolidated financial statements, the auditor should then apply the directions in Appendix B. (Paragraph 87; see Release No. 34-49544 (SEC 2004), Fed. Sec. L. Rep. ¶ 87,203.)

For example, Paragraph B4 states that because of the importance of financially significant locations or business units, the auditor should evaluate management's documentation of and perform tests of controls over all relevant assertions related to significant accounts and disclosures at each financially significant location or business unit.

The combination of these directions means that the auditor should determine significant accounts and their relevant assertions based on the consolidated financial statements and perform tests of controls over all relevant assertions related to those significant accounts at each financially significant location or business unit for which the selected accounts are material at the account level. (See FAQ of June 23, 2004, Q. 16.)

Therefore, the auditor need not test controls over all relevant assertions for a significant account at a financially significant location when the significant account is immaterial. However, if accounts receivable is material at a location or business unit that is not otherwise considered financially significant, the auditor should test controls over all relevant assertions for accounts receivable at that location. (See FAQ of June 23, 2004, Q. 16.) This direction is consistent with the directions in paragraph B6 addressing locations or business units that involve specific risks.

The multi-location guidance in Appendix B also states that the auditor should test controls over a "large portion" of the company's operations and financial position. But Auditing Standard No. 2 does not set specific percentages that would achieve this level of testing.

During the comment period on the proposed standard, several commenters suggested that the standard should provide more specific directions regarding the evaluation of whether controls over a large portion of the company's operations and financial position had been tested, including establishing specific percentages.

But the Board decided that balancing auditor judgment with the consistency that would be enforced by increased specificity would be best served by this direction remaining principles-based. Therefore, Auditing Standard No. 2 leaves to the auditor's judgment the determination of what exactly constitutes a "large portion." (See FAQ of June 23, 2004, Q. 17.)

In addition, the evaluation of whether controls over a large portion of the company's operations or financial position have been tested should be made at the overall level, not at the individual significant account level. (Note to Paragraph B11; see Release No. 34-49544, supra.)

For example, auditors believing that they should test controls over X percent of some measure should evaluate whether they had tested controls over X percent of the company's consolidated operations or financial position (e.g., X percent of total assets or X percent of revenues) and not X percent of each individual significant account. (See FAQ of June 23, 2004, Q. 17.)

According to the PCAOB staff, the directions in Paragraph B11 that the auditor should test controls over a large portion of the company's operations or financial position are intended as a fail-safe to ensure that every audit of internal controls is supported by sufficient evidence. (See FAQ of June 23, 2004, Q. 18.) In no case should auditors find that they could merely test company-level controls without also testing controls over all relevant assertions related to significant accounts and disclosures.

The direction to test controls over a large portion of financial position or operations is easily satisfied at companies in which the auditor's testing of individual financially significant locations or business units clearly covers a large portion. However, in circumstances in which a company has a very large number of individually insignificant locations or business units, testing controls over 60 percent or 75 percent of the company's financial position or operations may result in an extensive amount of work, in which the auditor would test controls over hundreds and even thousands of individual locations to reach that type of percentage target.

In circumstances in which a company has a large number of individually insignificant locations or business units and management asserts to the auditor that controls have been documented and are effective at all locations or business units, the auditor may satisfy the directions in Paragraph B11 by testing a representative sample of the company's locations or business units. (See FAQ of June 23, 2004, Q. 18.)

¶ 711

The auditor may select the representative sample either statistically or nonstatistically. However, the locations or business units should be selected in such a way that the sample is expected to be representative of the entire population.

Also, particularly in the case of a non-statistical sample, the auditor's sampling will be based on the expectation of no, or very few, control testing exceptions. In such circumstances, because of the nature of the sample and the control testing involved, the auditor will not have an accurate basis on which to extrapolate an error or exception rate that is more than negligible.

Furthermore, the existence of testing exceptions would not support management's assertion that controls had been documented and were effective at all locations or business units.

Therefore, if the auditor elects to use a representative sample in these circumstances and encounters testing exceptions within the sample that exceed a negligible rate, the auditor might decide that testing controls over a very large number of individual locations or business units is necessary to adequately support his or her opinion.

SEC Scope Limitations

Paragraphs B16 and B17 of Auditing Standard No. 2 provide direction to the auditor in situations in which the SEC allows management to limit its assessment of internal control over financial reporting by excluding certain entities. Generally, the auditor may limit the audit in the same manner.

While the SEC typically expects management's report on internal control over financial reporting to include controls at all consolidated entities, the Commission also recognizes that it might not always be possible to conduct an assessment of an acquired business's internal controls in the period between the consummation date of the purchase and the date of management's assessment.

In such instances, the SEC staff would not object to management referring in the report to a discussion in the company's Form 10-K regarding the scope of the assessment and to such disclosure noting that management excluded the acquired business from management's report on internal control over financial reporting. (See FAQ of June 23, Q. 3.) If such a reference is made, however, management must identify the acquired business excluded and indicate the significance of the acquired business to the company's consolidated financial statements.

Moreover, despite management's exclusion of an acquired business's internal controls from its annual assessment, a company must disclose any material change to its internal controls due to the acquisition. In addition, the period in which management may omit an assessment of an acquired business's internal controls from its overall assessment of the company's internal controls may not extend beyond one year from the date of acquisition, nor may such assessment be omitted from more than one annual management report on internal control over financial reporting.

While in these situations the auditor's opinion would not be affected by a scope limitation, the PCAOB staff advises auditors to include, either in an additional explanatory paragraph or as part of the scope paragraph in their report, a disclosure similar to management's regarding the exclusion of an entity from the scope of both management's assessment and the auditor's audit of internal control over financial reporting. (See FAQ of June 23, 2004, Q. 19.)

It should be remembered that the standard also directs the auditor to evaluate the reasonableness of management's conclusion that the situation meets the criteria of the SEC's allowed exclusion and the appropriateness of any required disclosure related to such limitation. (Paragraph B16; see Release No. 34-49544, supra.)

Auditors who conclude that management's disclosure about the situation requires modification should communicate the matter to the appropriate level of management as soon as practicable and, if no response is forthcoming within a reasonable time, the audit committee should be informed. (Paragraphs 204 and 205.) Further, if management and the audit committee do not respond appropriately, auditors should modify their report on the audit of internal control over financial reporting to include an explanatory paragraph describing the reasons why they believe management's disclosure should be modified. (Paragraph B16.)

CHAPTER 8

USING WORK OF OTHERS

Introduction . . . . ¶ 801
Evaluating Controls . . . . ¶ 802
Testing Work of Others . . . . ¶ 803
Evaluating Fraud Risks . . . . ¶ 804

¶ 801   Introduction

Auditing Standard No. 2 envisions allowing the auditor to make use of the work of others, including the inside auditors. But while the work of others may be used, the auditor's own work must provide the principal evidence for the audit opinion. (Paragraph 108; see Release No. 34-49544 (SEC 2004), FED. SEC. L. REP. ¶ 87,203.)

Similarly, auditors must obtain sufficient evidence to support their opinion. Judgments about the sufficiency of evidence obtained and other factors affecting the auditor's opinion, such as the significance of identified control deficiencies, should be those of the auditor. (Paragraph 110; see Release No. 34-49544, supra.)

Principal Evidence Provision

The principal evidence provision of the standard is very important since the Board views it as critical in preventing overreliance on the work of others in an audit of internal control over financial reporting. (Paragraph E44; see Release No. 34-49544, supra.)

The requirement for auditors to perform enough of the control testing themselves so that their own work provides the principal evidence for their opinion is of paramount importance to the auditor's assurance providing the level of reliability that investors expect.

Although the standard requires that auditors obtain the principal evidence supporting their opinions through procedures they performed, the PCAOB chairman has assured that this is not intended to imply that an internal auditor's work lacks value. Moreover, the Board does not want to discourage internal auditors from testing and evaluating internal controls, especially those related to the timely prevention and detection of fraud. (See remarks of Chairman William McDonough to the Maryland Society of CPAs, June 25, 2004.)

The auditor should test some of the work performed by others to evaluate the quality and effectiveness of their work. But the staff has cautioned that the auditor's testing of the work of others is not considered to be part of the principal evidence obtained by the auditor. (See staff interpretation of June 23, 2004, Q. 21.)

However, the auditor's independent testing of similar controls not tested by others may, in these circumstances, be considered as work performed by the auditor when evaluating whether the auditor obtained the principal evidence supporting his or her opinion, but only if these independent tests are not for the purpose of assessing the quality and effectiveness of the work of others.

If the independent tests are for the purpose of assessing the quality and effectiveness of others' work, then the independent tests should not be considered as work performed by the auditor when evaluating whether the auditor obtained the principal evidence supporting his or her opinion. (See staff interpretation of June 23, 2004, Q. 22.)

Because the amount of work related to obtaining sufficient evidence to support an opinion about the effectiveness of controls is not susceptible to precise measurement, the auditor's judgment about whether he or she has obtained the principal evidence for the opinion will be qualitative as well as quantitative. For example, auditors might give more weight to work performed on pervasive controls and in areas such as the control environment than on other controls, such as controls over low-risk, routine transactions.

Auditors may use the work of others to alter the nature, timing, or extent of the work they otherwise would have performed. For these purposes, the work of others includes relevant work performed by internal auditors, other company personnel, and third parties working under the direction of management or the audit committee that provides information about the effectiveness of internal control over financial reporting. (Paragraph 108; see Release No. 34-49544, supra.)

But also note that evidence obtained through the auditor's direct personal knowledge, observation, and inspection is generally more persuasive than information obtained indirectly from others, such as from internal auditors, other company personnel, or third parties working under the direction of management. (Paragraph 110.)

Auditing Standard No. 2 establishes a framework for using the work of others based on evaluating the nature of the controls, evaluating the competence and objectivity of the individuals who performed the work, and testing some of the work performed by others to evaluate the quality and effectiveness of their work.

Within this framework, the amount of testing of others' work should suffice to enable the auditor to evaluate the overall quality and effectiveness of their work. Auditing Standard No. 2 provides flexibility in this regard. Thus, testing the work of others in every significant account in which the auditor plans to use their work is not required. (See Staff Interpretation of June 23, 2004, Q. 20.)

Furthermore, if the auditor believes that extensive testing of the work of others is necessary in every area in which the auditor plans to use their work, the auditor should consider the directions in Paragraph 124 of Auditing Standard No. 2. Those directions state that the auditor should also assess whether the evaluation of the quality and effectiveness of the work of others has an effect on the auditor's conclusions about the competence and objectivity of the individuals performing the work.

If the auditor determines the need to test the work of others to a high degree, the auditor should consider whether his or her original assessment of their competence and objectivity is correct.

The auditor must evaluate whether to use the work performed by others in the audit of internal control over financial reporting. To determine the extent to which the auditor may use others' work, the auditor should:

● Evaluate the nature of the controls subjected to the work of others;

● Evaluate the competence and objectivity of the individuals who performed the work; and

● Test some of the work performed by others to evaluate the quality and effectiveness of their work. (Paragraph 109; see Release No. 34-49544, supra.)

These three important factors are discussed elsewhere (see ¶ 802).

¶ 802   Evaluating Controls

The auditor should evaluate the following factors when evaluating the nature of the controls subjected to the work of others:

● The materiality of the accounts and disclosures that the control addresses and the risk of material misstatement;

● The degree of judgment required to evaluate the operating effectiveness of the control, which is the degree to which the evaluation of the effectiveness of the control requires evaluation of subjective factors rather than objective testing;

● The pervasiveness of the control;

● The level of judgment or estimation required in the account or disclosure; and

● The potential for management override of the control. (Auditing Standard No. 2, Paragraph 112; see Release No. 34-49544 (SEC 2004), FED. SEC. L. REP. ¶ 87,203.)

As these factors increase in significance, the need for auditors to perform their own work on those controls increases. As these factors decrease in significance, the need for auditors to perform their own work on those controls decreases.

The Board advises that auditors should not use the work of others to reduce the amount of work they perform on controls in the control environment. Auditors should, however, consider the results of work performed in this area by others because it might indicate the need for the auditors to increase their own work. The control environment encompasses the following factors:

● Integrity and ethical values;

● Commitment to competence;

● Board of directors or audit committee participation;

● Management's philosophy and operating style;

● Organizational structure;

● Assignment of authority and responsibility; and

● Human resource policies and procedures. (Paragraph 114; see Release No. 34-49544, supra.)

Controls that are part of the control environment include, but are not limited to, controls specifically established to prevent and detect fraud that is at least reasonably possible to result in material misstatement of the financial statements. The standard defines the term "reasonably possible" by reference to FASB Statement No. 5, under which reasonably possible means that the chance of the future event occurring is more than remote but less than likely.

Although the standard envisions auditors performing walkthroughs themselves because of the degree of judgment required, the Board said that, to provide additional evidence, auditors may also review the work of others who have performed and documented walkthroughs.

Evaluating Competency and Objectivity of Others

The extent to which the auditor may use the work of others depends on the degree of competence and objectivity of the individuals performing the work. The higher the degree of competence and objectivity, the greater use the auditor may make of the work. Conversely, the lower the degree of competence and objectivity, the less use the auditor may make of the work.

Also, the auditor should not use the work of individuals who have a low degree of objectivity, regardless of their level of competence. Likewise, the auditor should not use the work of individuals who have a low level of competence regardless of their degree of objectivity. The following factors should be used in determining the competency of other individuals performing the tests of controls:

- Their education and professional experience;

- Their professional certification and continuing education;

- Practices regarding the assignment of individuals to work areas;

- Supervision and review of their activities;

- Quality of the documentation of their work, including reports and recommendations; and

- Performance evaluations. (Paragraph 119; see Release No. 34-49544, supra.)

In determining the objectivity of other individuals performing the tests of controls, the auditor should consider two broad factors. First, the auditor should consider the organizational status of the individuals responsible for the work of others in testing controls (the testing authority), including whether:

- the testing authority reports to an officer of sufficient status to ensure sufficient testing coverage and action on the findings and recommendations of the individuals performing the testing.

- the testing authority has direct access and reportsregularly to the board of directors or the audit committee.

- the board of directors or the audit committee overseesemployment decisions relating to the testing authority.

Second, the auditor should consider policies to maintain the individuals' objectivity about the areas being tested. These include policies prohibiting individuals from testing controls in areas: (i) in which relatives are employed in important or internal control-sensitive positions; or (ii) to which they were recently assigned or are scheduled to be assigned upon completion of their controls testing responsibilities. (Paragraph 120; see Release No. 34-49544, supra.)

Internal auditors normally should have greater competence with regard to internal control over financial reporting and objectivity than other company personnel. Therefore, the auditor may be able to use their work to a greater extent than the work of other company personnel. This would particularly be true in the case of internal auditors who follow the International Standards for the Professional Practice of Internal Auditing issued by the Institute of Internal Auditors.

If internal auditors have performed an extensive amount of relevant work and the auditor determines they possess a high degree of competence and objectivity, the auditor could use their work to the greatest extent an auditor could use the work of others.

But the Board also cautioned that the independent auditor should use the work of the internal auditors to a much lesser extent if: (1) the internal audit function reports solely to management, since this would reduce internal auditors' objectivity; or (2) limited resources allocated to the internal audit function result in limited testing procedures on its part or reduced competency of the internal auditors. (Paragraph 121; see Release No. 34-49544, supra.)

¶ 803   Testing Work of Others

The auditor should test some of the work of others to evaluate the quality and effectiveness of the work. Auditing Standard No. 2 allows these tests to be accomplished either by testing: (1) some of the controls that others tested; or (2) similar controls not actually tested by others.

The nature and extent of these tests depend on the effect of the work of others on the auditor's procedures but should be sufficient to enable the auditor to make an evaluation of the overall quality and effectiveness of the work the auditor is considering. Auditors should also assess whether this evaluation has an effect on their conclusions about the competence and objectivity of the individuals performing the work.

In evaluating the quality and effectiveness of the work of others, the auditor should evaluate such factors as to whether:

● the scope of work is appropriate to meet the objectives;

● the work programs are adequate;

● the work performed is adequately documented, including evidence of supervision and review;

● the conclusions are appropriate in the circumstances; and

● the reports are consistent with the results of the work performed. (Auditing Standard No. 2, Paragraph 125; see Release No. 34-49544 (SEC 2004), FED. SEC. L. REP. ¶ 87,203.)

Specific Applications

The Board has advised on how to apply its directions in five discrete areas of internal control over financial reporting: (1) period-end financial reporting; (2) information technology general controls; (3) management self-assessment of controls; (4) controls over the calculation of depreciation of fixed assets; and (5) alternating tests of controls. (Paragraph 126; see Release No. 34-49544, supra.) These areas are discussed separately below:

Period-end financial reporting

When it comes to controls over the period-end financial reporting process, the auditor could use the work of the internal auditors to some extent, but should not use the work of other company personnel. The Board's position is based on the fact that many of the controls over the period-end financial reporting process address significant risks of misstatement of the accounts and disclosures in the annual and quarterly financial statements and may require significant judgment to evaluate their operating effectiveness. In addition, they may have a higher potential for management override and may affect accounts that require a high level of judgment or estimation.

Thus, auditors could determine that, based on the nature of controls over the period-end financial reporting process, they would need to perform more of the tests of those controls themselves.

Information technology

Regarding information technology controls, program change controls over routine maintenance changes may have a highly pervasive effect, yet involve a low degree of judgment in evaluating their operating effectiveness. They can also be subjected to objective testing, and they have a low potential for management override.

Thus, the auditor could determine that, based on the nature of these program change controls, the work of others could be used to a moderate extent so long as the degree of competence and objectivity of the individuals performing the test is at an appropriate level.

On the other hand, controls to detect attempts to override controls that prevent unauthorized journal entries from being posted may have a highly pervasive effect and may involve a high degree of subjective judgment in evaluating their operating effectiveness.

Thus, auditors could determine that, based on the nature of these controls over systems access, they would need to perform more of the tests themselves. Further, because of the nature of these controls, the work of others should be used only if the degree of competence and objectivity of the individuals performing the tests is high.

Management's self-assessment

Although management is permitted to test the operating effectiveness of controls using a self-assessment process, the auditor should not use their work. Since the assessment is made by the same personnel who are responsible for performing the control, they will lack sufficient objectivity.

Calculating depreciation of fixed assets

Controls over the calculation of depreciation of fixed assets are usually not pervasive, involve a low degree of judgment in evaluating their operating effectiveness, and can be subjected to objective testing. This being the case, and if there is a low potential for management override, the auditor could use the work of others to a large extent (perhaps entirely) so long as the degree of competence and objectivity of the individuals performing the test is at an appropriate level.

Alternating tests

Similarly, many of the controls over accounts payable, including controls over cash disbursements, are usually not pervasive, involve a low degree of judgment in evaluating their operating effectiveness, can be subjected to objective testing, and have a low potential for management override. Thus, the auditor could use the work of others to a large extent (perhaps entirely) so long as the degree of competence and objectivity of the individuals performing the test is at an appropriate level.

However, if the company recently implemented a major informationtechnology change that significantly affected controls over cash disbursements, the auditor might decide to use the work of others to a lesser extent in the audit immediately following the information technology change and then return, in subsequent years, to using the work of others to a large extent in this area.

As another example, auditors might use the work of others for testing controls over the depreciation of fixed assets for several years' audits but decide one year to perform some extent of the work themselves to gain an understanding of these controls beyond that provided by a walkthrough. (Paragraph 126; see Release No. 34-49544, supra.)

¶ 804   Evaluating Fraud Risks

The auditor's evaluation of controls in an audit of internal control over financial reporting is interrelated with the auditor's evaluation of fraud risks in a financial statement audit as required by AU Section 316. (Auditing Standard No. 2, Paragraph 26; see Release No. 34-49544 (SEC 2004), FED. SEC. L. REP. ¶ 87,203.)

AU Section 316 requires, among other things, that the auditor identify risks that may result in a material misstatement of the financial statements due to fraud and that the auditor should respond to those identified risks. AU Section 316 emphasizes that the auditor's response to the risks of material misstatement due to fraud involves the application of professional skepticism when gathering and evaluating evidence.

Section 316 establishes a presumption that there is a risk of material misstatement due to fraud relating to revenue recognition. If the auditor does not overcome this presumption, as would frequently be the case with, for example, software revenue recognition, the auditor should test the controls specifically established to prevent and detect fraud related to a material misstatement of the company's revenue recognition himself or herself. (See staff interpretation of June 23, 2004, Q. 23.)

Moreover, because material misstatement due to fraud often involves manipulation of the financial reporting process by management, AU Section

316 also requires the auditor to review journal entries and other adjustments for evidence of material misstatement due to fraud. Paragraph 112 of Auditing Standard No. 2 includes as one of the factors that the auditor should evaluate when evaluating the nature of the controls subjected to the work of others the potential for management override of the control. (See Release No. 34-49544 (SEC 2004), FED. SEC. L. REP. ¶ 87,203.)

Taken together, these directions mean that obtaining the understanding of the design of controls over journal entries and other adjustments and determining whether they are suitably designed and have been placed in operation, as required by AU Section 316, and performing any associated testing of those controls that the auditor determines is necessary when auditing internal control over financial reporting under Auditing Standard No. 2, should be performed by the auditor himself or herself.

However, Auditing Standard No. 2 emphasizes that, although the auditor should not use the work of others in this situation, the auditor should consider the results of work performed in the area by others because it might indicate the need for the auditor to increase his or her work.

CHAPTER 9

FORMING OPINION ON CONTROL EFFECTIVENESS

Introduction .... ¶ 901

Evaluating Deficiencies .... ¶ 902

Indicator of Material Weakness .... ¶ 903

Written Representations Requirement .... ¶ 904

¶ 901   Introduction

When forming an opinion on internal control over financial reporting, the auditor should evaluate all evidence obtained from all sources, including:

● The adequacy of management's assessment and the results of the auditor's evaluation of the design and tests of operating effectiveness of controls;

● The negative results of substantive procedures performed during the financial statement audit; and

● Any identified control deficiencies.

As part of this evaluation, the auditor should review all reports issued during the year by internal audit that address controls related to internal control over financial reporting and evaluate any control deficiencies identified in those reports. This review should include reports issued by internal audit as a result of operational audits or specific reviews of key processes if those reports address controls related to internal control over financial reporting.

Unqualified Opinions

The auditor may issue an unqualified opinion only when: (1) there are no identified material weaknesses; and (2) there have been no restrictions on the scope of the auditor's work. The existence of a material weakness requires the auditor to express an adverse opinion on the effectiveness of internal control over financial reporting. (Paragraph 175; see Release No. 34-49544 (SEC 2004), FED. SEC. L. REP. ¶ 87,203.)

The existence of a scope limitation requires the auditor to express a qualified opinion or a disclaimer of opinion, depending on the significance of the limitation. (Paragraph 178).

¶ 902   Evaluating Deficiencies

The auditor must evaluate identified control deficiencies and determine whether the deficiencies, individually or in combination, are significant deficiencies or material weaknesses. The evaluation of the significance of a deficiency should include both quantitative and qualitative factors. (Auditing Standard No. 2, Paragraph 130; see Release No. 34-49544 (SEC 2004), FED. SEC. L. REP. ¶ 87,203.) Initially, the auditor should evaluate the significance of a deficiency in internal controls by determining:

● The likelihood that a deficiency or combination of deficiencies could result in a misstatement of an account balance or disclosure; and

● The magnitude of the potential misstatement resulting from the deficiency. (Paragraph 131; see Release No. 34-49544, supra.)

Note that the significance of a deficiency depends on the potential for a misstatement not in whether a misstatement has actually occurred.

Several factors affect the likelihood that a deficiency, or a combination of deficiencies, could result in a misstatement of an account balance or disclosure. The factors include, but are not limited to, the following:

● The nature of the financial statement accounts, disclosures, and assertions involved; for example, suspense accounts and related party transactions involve greater risk.

● The susceptibility of the related assets or liability to loss or fraud.

● The subjectivity, complexity, or extent of judgment required to determine the amount involved; for example, greater subjectivity, complexity, or judgment, such as that related to accounting estimates, increases risk.

● The cause and frequency of known or detected exceptions for the operating effectiveness of a control; for example, a control with an observed non-negligible deviation rate is a deficiency.

● The interaction or relationship of the control with other controls; that is, are the controls interdependent or redundant.

● The interaction of the deficiencies; for example, whether two deficiencies could affect the same financial statement accounts.

● The possible future consequences of the deficiency. (Paragraph 133; see Release No. 34-49544, supra.)

When evaluating the likelihood that a deficiency could result in a misstatement, the Board advises the auditor to evaluate how the controls interact with other controls. There are controls, such as IT general controls, on which other controls depend. Some controls function together as a group of controls, while others overlap in the sense that they achieve the same objective. (Paragraph 134).

The Board has listed at least two non-exclusive factors affecting the magnitude of the misstatement that could result from a control deficiency: (1) the financial statement amounts or total of transactions exposed to the deficiency; and (2) the volume of activity in the account balance or class of transactions exposed to the deficiency that has occurred in the current period or that is expected in future periods. (Paragraph 135; see Release No. 34-49544, supra.)

In evaluating the magnitude of the potential misstatement, the auditor should recognize that the maximum amount that an account balance or total of transactions can be overstated is generally the recorded amount. However, the recorded amount is not a limitation on the amount of potential understatement. The auditor should also recognize that the risk of misstatement might be different for the maximum possible misstatement than for lesser possible amounts. (Paragraph 136.)

Significance of Deficiency

When evaluating the significance of a deficiency in internal control over financial reporting, the auditor also should determine the level of detail and degree of assurance that would satisfy prudent officials in the conduct of their own affairs that they have reasonable assurance that transactions are recorded as necessary to permit the preparation of financial statements in conformity with generally accepted accounting principles. (Paragraph 137.)

If the auditor determines that the deficiency would prevent prudent officials in the conduct of their own affairs from concluding that they have reasonable assurance, the Board advises, the auditor should deem the deficiency to be at least a significant deficiency. Here the Board refers to SEC Staff Accounting Bulletin Topic 1M2 on immaterial misstatements that are intentional for the level of detail and degree of assurance that would satisfy prudent officials in the conduct of their own affairs.

If a deficiency is determined to be a significant deficiency, the auditor must further evaluate it to determine whether individually, or in combination with other deficiencies, the deficiency is a material weakness.

The Board has noted that inadequate documentation of the design of controls and the absence of sufficient documented evidence to support management's assessment of the operating effectiveness of internal control over financial reporting are control deficiencies. As with other control deficiencies, the auditor should evaluate these deficiencies as to their significance. (Paragraph 138.)

Deficiencies in the following areas will generally be at least significant deficiencies in internal control over financial reporting:

● Controls over the selection and application of accounting policies that are in conformity with GAAP;

● Antifraud programs and controls;

● Controls over non-routine and non-systemic transactions;

● Controls over the period-end financial reporting process, including controls over procedures used to enter transaction totals into the Identification by general ledger; initiate, authorize, record, and process journal entries into the general ledger; and record recurring and nonrecurring adjustments to the financial statements. (Paragraph 139.)

¶ 903   Indicator of Material Weakness

Certain circumstances should be regarded as at least a significant deficiency and as a strong indicator that a material weakness in internal control over financial reporting exists. (Auditing Standard No. 2, Paragraph 140; see Release No. 34-49544 (SEC 2004), Fed. Sec. L. Rep. ¶ 87,203.) These include:

● The restatement of previously issued financial statements to reflect the correction of a misstatement. This item includes misstatements due to error or fraud; but not restatements to reflect a change in accounting principle to comply with a new accounting principle or a voluntary change from one generally accepted accounting principle to another.

● The auditor's identification of a material misstatement in financial statements in the current period that was not initially identified by the company's internal control over financial reporting. Note that this is a strong indicator of a material weakness even if management subsequently corrects the misstatement.

● Ineffective audit committee oversight of the company's external financial reporting and internal control over financial reporting.

● The internal audit function or the risk assessment function is ineffective at a company for which such a function needs to be effective for the company to have an effective monitoring or risk assessment component, such as for very large or highly complex companies.

● For complex entities in highly regulated industries, an ineffective regulatory compliance function. This relates solely to those aspects of the ineffective regulatory compliance function in which associated violations of laws and regulations could have a material effect on the reliability of financial reporting.

● Identification of fraud of any magnitude on the part of senior management. For this purpose, senior management includes the principal executive and financial officers signing the company's Section 302 certifications, as well other members of management who play a significant role in the financial reporting prices.

● Significant deficiencies communicated to management and the audit committee remain uncorrected after some reasonable period of time.

● An ineffective control environment

Staff Guidance

The PCAOB staff has provided detailed interpretation on when an auditor identifies a material misstatement in financial statements in the current period that was not initially identified by the company's internal controls. The inclusion of this circumstance as a significant deficiency and a strong indicator of a material weakness emphasizes that a company must have effective internal control over financial reporting on its own. (See FAQ of June 23, 2004 Q. 7).

More specifically, the results of auditing procedures cannot be considered when evaluating whether the company's internal controls provide reasonable assurance that its financial statements will be presented fairly in accordance with GAAP.

There are a variety of ways that a company can emphasize that it, rather than the auditor, is responsible for the financial statements and that the company has effective controls surrounding the preparation of financial statements.

Modifying the traditional audit process such that the company provides the auditor with only a single draft of the financial statements to audit when the company believes that all its controls over the preparation of the financial statements have fully operated is one way to demonstrate management's responsibility and to be clear that all the company's controls have operated.

The staff recognizes, however, that this process is not necessarily what was expected to result from the implementation of Auditing Standard No. 2 since such might make it difficult for some companies to meet the accelerated filing deadlines for their annual reports. More importantly, such a process, combined with the accelerated filing deadlines, might put the auditor under significant pressure to complete the audit of the financial statements in too short a time period thereby impairing, rather than improving, audit quality.

Therefore, the staff contemplates the necessity for some type of information-sharing on a timely basis between management and the auditor. In that spirit, a company may share interim drafts of the financial statements with the auditor.

The company can minimize the risk that auditors would determine that their involvement in this process might represent a significant deficiency or material weakness through clear communications (either written or oral) with the auditor about: (1) the state of completion of the financial statements; (2) the extent of controls that had operated or not operated at the time; and (3) the purpose for which the company was giving the draft financial statements to the auditor.

Example 1—A company might give the auditor draft financial statements to audit that lack two notes required by GAAP. Absent any communication from the company to clearly indicate recognition that two specific required notes are lacking, the auditor might determine that the lack of those notes constitutes a material misstatement of the financial statements that represents a significant deficiency and is a strong indicator of a material weakness.

On the other hand, if the company makes it clear when it provides the draft financial statements to the auditor that two specific required notes are lacking and that those completed notes will be provided at a later time, the auditor would not consider their omission at that time a material misstatement of the financial statements.

Example 2—A company might release a partially completed note to the auditor and make clear that the company's process for preparing the numerical information included in a related table is complete and, therefore, that the company considers the numerical information to be fairly stated even though it has not yet completed the text of the note. At the same time, the company might indicate that the auditor should not yet subject the entire note to audit, but only the table.

In this case, the auditor would evaluate only the numerical information in the table and the company's process to complete the table. However, an auditor identifying a misstatement of the information in the table should consider that circumstance a misstatement of the financial statements. If the auditor determines that the misstatement is material, a significant deficiency as well as a strong indicator of a material weakness would exist.

¶ 904   Written Representations Requirement

In an audit of internal control over financial reporting, the auditor should obtain certain written representations from management. (Auditing Standard No. 2, Paragraph 142; see Release No. 34-49544 (SEC 2004), Fed. Sec. L. Rep. ¶ 87,203.) Specifically, the auditor should obtain a written representation:

● Acknowledging management's responsibility for maintaining effective internal control over financial reporting;

● Stating that management has performed an assessment of the effectiveness of the company's internal control over financial reporting and specifying the control criteria;

● Stating that management did not use the auditor's procedures performed during the audits of internal control over financial reporting or the financial statements as part of the basis for management's assessment of the effectiveness of internal control over financial reporting;

● Stating management's conclusion about the effectiveness of the company's internal control over financial reporting based on the control criteria as of a specified date;

● Stating that management has disclosed to the auditor all deficiencies in the design or operation of internal control over financial reporting identified as part of management's assessment, including separately disclosing to the auditor all such deficiencies that it believes to be significant deficiencies or material weaknesses in internal control over financial reporting;

● Describing any material fraud and any other fraud that, although not material, involves senior management or management or other employees who have a significant role in the company's internal control over financial reporting;

● Stating whether control deficiencies identified and communicated to the audit committee during previous engagements have been resolved, and specifically identifying any that have not; and

● Stating whether there were, subsequent to the date being reported on, any changes in internal control over financial reporting or other factors that might significantly affect internal control over financial reporting, including any corrective actions taken by management with regard to significant deficiencies and material weaknesses.

The failure to obtain written representations from management, including management's refusal to furnish them, constitutes a limitation on the scope of the audit sufficient to preclude an unqualified opinion. When management limits the scope of the audit, the auditor should either withdraw from the engagement or disclaim an opinion. Further, auditors should evaluate the effects of management's refusal on their ability to rely on other representations, including, if applicable, representations obtained in an audit of the company's financial statements.

CHAPTER 10

RELATIONSHIP OF CONTROL AUDIT TO FINANCIAL STATEMENT AUDIT

Introduction .... ¶ 1001
Test of Controls (Internal Controls Audit)........... ¶ 1002
Test of Controls (Financial Statement Audit) .... ¶ 1003
Effect of Test of Controls .... ¶ 1004
Effect of Substantive Procedures................. ¶ 1005
Documentation Requirements .... ¶ 1006

¶ 1001   Introduction

The Board believes that the audit of internal control over financial reporting should be integrated with the audit of the financial statements. The objectives of the procedures for the audits are not identical, however, and the auditor must plan and perform the work to achieve the objectives of both audits. (Auditing Standard No. 2, Paragraphs 145-146; see Release No. 34-49544 (SEC 2004), FED. SEC. L. REP. ¶ 87,203.)

The understanding of internal control over financial reporting the auditor obtains and the procedures the auditor performs for purposes of expressing an opinion on management's assessment are interrelated with the internal control over financial reporting understanding the auditor obtains and procedures the auditor performs to assess control risk for purposes of expressing an opinion on the financial statements. As a result, it is efficient for the auditor to coordinate obtaining the understanding and performing the procedures.

¶ 1002   Test of Controls (Internal Controls Audit)

The objective of the tests of controls in an audit of internal control over financial reporting is to obtain evidence about the effectiveness of controls to support the auditor's opinion on whether management's assessment of the effectiveness of the company's internal controls is fairly stated. The auditor's opinion relates to the effectiveness of the company's internal control over financial reporting as of a point in time and taken as a whole. (Auditing Standard No. 2, Paragraph 147; see Release No. 34-49544 (SEC 2004), FED. SEC. L. REP. ¶ 87,203.)

To express an opinion on internal control over financial reporting effectiveness as of a point in time, the auditor should obtain evidence that internal control over financial reporting has operated effectively for a sufficient period of time, which may be less than the entire period (ordinarily one year) covered by the company's financial statements.

To express an opinion on internal control over financial reporting effectiveness taken as a whole, the auditor must obtain evidence about the effectiveness of controls over all relevant assertions related to all significant accounts and disclosures in the financial statements. (Paragraph 148; see Release No. 34-49544, supra.) This requires that auditors test the design and operating effectiveness of controls they ordinarily would not test if expressing an opinion only on the financial statements.

When concluding on the effectiveness of internal controls for purposes of expressing an opinion on management's assessment, the auditor should incorporate the results of any additional tests of controls performed to achieve the objective related to expressing an opinion on the financial statements. (Paragraph 149; see Release No. 34-49544, supra.)

¶ 1003   Test of Controls (Financial Statement Audit)

To express an opinion on the financial statements, the auditor ordinarily performs tests of controls and substantive procedures. The objective of the tests of controls the auditor performs for this purpose is to assess control risk.

To assess control risk for specific financial statement assertions at less than the maximum, the auditor must obtain evidence that the relevant controls operated effectively during the entire period on which the auditor plans to place reliance on those controls. However, the auditor need not assess control risk at less than the maximum for all relevant assertions and, for a variety of reasons, the auditor may choose not to do so. (Auditing Standard No. 2, Paragraph 150; see Release No. 34-49544 (SEC 2004), FED. SEC. L. REP. ¶ 87,203.)

When concluding on the effectiveness of controls for the purpose of assessing control risk, the auditor also should evaluate the results of any additional tests of controls performed to achieve the objective related to expressing an opinion on management's assessment, as discussed above. (Paragraph 151; see Release No. 34-49544, supra.)

Consideration of these results may require the auditor to alter the nature, timing, and extent of substantive procedures and to plan and perform further tests of controls, particularly in response to identified control deficiencies.

¶ 1004   Effect of Tests of Controls

Regardless of the assessed level of control risk or the assessed risk of material misstatement in connection with the audit of the financial statements, the auditor should perform substantive procedures for all relevant assertions related to all significant accounts and disclosures. (Auditing Standard No. 2, Paragraph 152; see Release No. 34-49544 (SEC 2004), FED. SEC. L. REP. ¶ 87,203.)

Note that performing procedures to express an opinion on internal control over financial reporting does not diminish this requirement.

The substantive procedures that the auditor should perform consist of tests of details of transactions and balances and analytical procedures. Before using the results obtained from substantive analytical procedures, the auditor should either test the design and operating effectiveness of controls over financial information used in the substantive analytical procedures or perform other procedures to support the completeness and accuracy of the underlying information. (Paragraph 153; see Release No. 34-49544, supra.)

For significant risks of material misstatement, it is unlikely that audit evidence obtained from substantive analytical procedures alone will be sufficient.

When designing substantive analytical procedures, the auditor also should evaluate the risk of management override of controls. As part of this process, the auditor should evaluate whether such an override might have allowed adjustments outside of the normal period-end financial reporting process to have been made to the financial statements. (Paragraph 154; see Release No. 34-49544, supra.)

Such adjustments might have resulted in artificial changes to the financial statement relationships being analyzed, causing the auditor to draw erroneous conclusions. For this reason, the Board has reasoned, substantive analytical procedures alone are not well suited to detecting fraud.

According to the Board, the auditor's substantive procedures must include reconciling the financial statements to the accounting records. The auditor's substantive procedures also should include examining material adjustments made during the course of preparing the financial statements. (Paragraph 155; see Release No. 34-49544, supra.)

In addition, other auditing standards require auditors to perform specific tests of details in the financial statement audit. For instance, AU Section 316 requires the auditor to perform certain tests of details to further address the risk of management override, whether or not a specific risk of fraud has been identified. Paragraph .34 of AU Section 330 states that there is a presumption that the auditor will request the confirmation of accounts receivable. Similarly, paragraph .01 of AU Section 331 states that observation of inventories is a generally accepted auditing procedure and that the auditor who issues an opinion without this procedure has the burden of justifying the opinion expressed.

Auditors identifying a control deficiency during the audit of internal controls should determine the effect on the nature, timing, and extent of substantive procedures to be performed to reduce the risk of material misstatement of the financial statements to an appropriately low level. (Paragraph 156; see Release No. 34-49544, supra.)

¶ 1005   Effect of Substantive Procedures

In an audit of internal control over financial reporting, the auditor should evaluate the effect of the findings of all substantive auditing procedures performed in the audit of financial statements on the effectiveness of internal control over financial statements. (Auditing Standard No. 2, Paragraph 157; see Release No. 34-49544 (SEC 2004), FED. SEC. L. REP. ¶ 87,203.) This evaluation should include, but not be limited to:

● The auditor's risk evaluations in connection with the selection and application of substantive procedures, especially those related to fraud;

● Findings with respect to illegal acts and related party transactions;

● Indications of management bias in making accounting estimates and in selecting accounting principles; and

● Misstatements detected by substantive procedures. The extent of such misstatements might alter the auditor's judgment about the effectivenessof controls.

Note however that the absence of misstatements detected by substantive procedures does not provide evidence that controls related to the assertion being tested are effective. (Paragraph 158; see Release No. 34-49544, supra.)

¶ 1006   Documentation Requirements

In addition to the documentation requirements in AU Section 339, auditors should document several other items. (Auditing Standard No. 2,

Paragraph 159; see Release No. 34-49544 (SEC 2004), FED. SEC. L. REP. ¶ 87,203.) Specifically, the auditor should document:

● The understanding obtained and the evaluation of the design of each of the five components of the company's internal control over financial reporting;

● The process used to determine significant accounts and disclosures and major classes of transactions, including the determination of the locations or business units at which to perform testing;

● The identification of the points at which misstatements related to relevant financial statement assertions could occur within significant accounts and disclosures and major classes of transactions;

● The extent to which the auditor relied on work performed by others as well as the auditor's assessment of their competence and objectivity;

● The evaluation of any deficiencies noted as a result of the auditor's testing; and

● Other findings that could result in a modification to the auditor's report.

For a company that has effective internal control over financial reporting, the auditor ordinarily will be able to perform sufficient testing of controls to be able to assess control risk for all relevant assertions related to significant accounts and disclosures at a low level. If, however, the auditor assesses control risk as other than low for certain assertions or significant accounts, the auditor should document the reasons for that conclusion. (Paragraph 160; see Release No. 34-49544, supra.) Examples of when it is appropriate to assess control risk as other than low include:

● When a control over a relevant assertion related to a significant account or disclosure was superseded late in the year and only the new control was tested for operating effectiveness.

● When a material weakness existed during the period under audit and was corrected by the end of the period.

The auditor also should document the effect of a conclusion that control risk is other than low for any relevant assertions related to any significant accounts in connection with the audit of the financial statements on his or her opinion on the audit of internal control over financial reporting. (Paragraph 161; see Release No. 34-49544, supra.)

CHAPTER 11

REPORTING ON INTERNAL CONTROLS

Introduction .... ¶ 1101
Auditor's Evaluation of Management Report........ ¶ 1102
Auditor's Report on Management's Assessment ...... ¶ 1103
Separate Reports .... ¶ 1104
Report Modifications .... ¶ 1105
Restrictions on Scope of Engagement .... ¶ 1106
Reference to Report of Other Auditors .... ¶ 1107
Subsequent Events.......................... ¶ 1108
Additional Information in Management's Report..... ¶ 1109
Effect of Adverse Opinion on Financial Audit .... ¶ 1110
Subsequent Discovery of Preexisting Information .... ¶ 1111

¶ 1101   Introduction

Management must include in its annual report its assessment of the effectiveness of the company's internal control over financial reporting in addition to its audited financial statements as of the end of the most recent fiscal year. Management's report on internal control over financial reporting must include the following:

● A statement of management's responsibility for establishing and maintaining adequate internal controls;

● A statement identifying the framework used by management to conduct the required assessment of the effectiveness of the company's internal controls;

● An assessment of the effectiveness of the company's internal controls as of the end of the most recent fiscal year, including an explicit statement as to whether the internal controls are effective; and

● A statement that the registered public accounting firm that audited the financial statements included in the annual report has issued an attestation report on management's assessment of the company's internal control over financial reporting. (See Regulation S-K Item 308.)

According to the Board, management should provide, both in its report on internal control over financial reporting and in its representation letter to the auditor, a written conclusion about the effectiveness of the company's internal control over financial reporting. (See Paragraph 163; see Release No. 34-49544 (SEC 2004), FED. SEC. L. REP. ¶ 87,203.)

The conclusion about the effectiveness of a company's internal control over financial reporting can take many forms; however, management must state a direct conclusion about whether the company's internal control over financial reporting is effective.

This standard, for example, includes the phrase, "Management's assessment that W Company maintained effective internal control over financial reporting as of [date]," to illustrate such a conclusion. Other phrases, such as, "management's assessment that W Company's internal control over financial reporting as of [date] is sufficient to meet the stated objectives," also might be used.

However, the conclusion should not be so subjective (for example, "very effective internal control") that people having competence in and using the same or similar criteria would not ordinarily be able to arrive at similar conclusions.

In addition, management cannot conclude that the company's internal control over financial reporting is effective if there are one or more material weaknesses. (See Regulation S-K Item 308(a)(3).) Further, management must disclose all material weaknesses that exist as of the end of the most recent fiscal year.

Management might be able to accurately represent that internal control over financial reporting, as of the end of the company's most recent fiscal year, is effective even if one or more material weaknesses existed during the period. To make this representation, management must have changed the internal control over financial reporting to eliminate the material weaknesses sufficiently in advance of the "as of" date and have satisfactorily tested the effectiveness over a period of time that is adequate for it to determine whether, as of the end of the fiscal year, the design and operation of internal control is effective (Paragraph 165; see Release No. 34-49544, supra.)

When the reason for a change in internal control over financial reporting is the correction of a material weakness, however, management and the auditor should evaluate whether the reason for the change and the circumstances surrounding the change are material information necessary to make the disclosure about the change not misleading in a filing subject to certification under the Exchange Act.

¶ 1102   Auditor's Evaluation of Management Report

With respect to management's report on its assessment, the auditor should evaluate certain matters. (Auditing Standard No. 2, Paragraph 166; see Release No. 34-49544 (SEC 2004), FED. SEC. L. REP. ¶ 87,203.) Specifically, the auditor should evaluate:

● Whether management has properly stated its responsibility for establishing and maintaining adequate internal control over financial reporting.

● Whether the framework used by management to conduct the evaluation is suitable. (The framework described in COSO constitutes a suitable and available framework.)

● Whether management's assessment of the effectiveness of internal control over financial reporting, as of the end of the company's most recent fiscal year, is free of material misstatement.

● Whether management has expressed its assessment in an acceptable form. The Board has declared as not acceptable a negative assurance statement indicating that, for example, "Nothing has come to management's attention to suggest that the company's internal control over financial reporting is not effective." Similarly, management is not permitted to conclude that the company's internal control over financial reporting is effective if there are one or more material weaknesses in the company's internal control over financial reporting.

● Whether material weaknesses identified in the company's internal control over financial reporting, if any, have been properly disclosed, including material weaknesses corrected during the period.

¶ 1103   Auditor's Report on Management's Assessment

The auditor's report on management's assessment of the effectiveness of internal control over financial reporting must contain certain elements. (Auditing Standard No. 2, Paragraph 167; see Release No. 34-49544 (SEC 2004), FED. SEC. L. REP. ¶ 87,203.) Specifically, the auditor's report must include:

● A title that includes the word independent;

● An identification of management's conclusion about the effectiveness of the company's internal controls as of a specified date based on the control criteria;

● An identification of the title of the management report that includes management's assessment (the auditor should use the same description of the company's internal control over financial reporting as management uses in its report);

● A statement that the assessment is the responsibility of management;

● A statement that the auditor's responsibility is to express an opinion on the assessment and an opinion on the company's internal control over financial reporting based on his or her audit;

● A definition of internal control over financial reporting as stated in paragraph 7 of Auditing Standard No. 2;

● A statement that the audit was conducted in accordance PCAOB standards;

● A statement that PCAOB standards require that the auditor plan and perform the audit to obtain reasonable assurance about whether effective internal control over financial was maintained in all material respects;

● A statement that an audit includes obtaining an understanding of internal controls, evaluating management's assessment, testing and evaluating the design and operating effectiveness of internal controls, and performing such other procedures as the auditor considered necessary in the circumstances;

● A statement that the auditor believes the audit provides a reasonable basis for his or her opinions;

● A paragraph stating that, because of inherent limitations, internal controls may not prevent or detect misstatements and that projections of any evaluation of effectiveness to future periods are subject to the risk that controls may become inadequate because of changes in conditions, or that the degree of compliance with the policies or procedures may deteriorate;

● The auditor's opinion on whether management's assessment of the effectiveness of the company's internal control over financial reporting as of the specified date is fairly stated, in all material respects, based on the control criteria;

● The auditor's opinion on whether the company maintained, in all material respects, effective internal controls as of the specified date, based on the control criteria;

● The manual or printed signature of the auditor's firm;

● The city and state (or city and country, in the case of non-U.S. auditors) from which the auditor's report has been issued; and

● The date of the audit report.

Combined Reports

The auditor may choose to issue a combined report containing both an opinion on the financial statements and the opinion on internal control over financial reporting. (Paragraph 169; see Release No. 34-49544 (SEC 2004), FED. SEC. L. REP. ¶ 87,203.) When the auditor elects to issue a combined report, the audit opinion will address multiple reporting periods for the financial statements presented but only the end of the most recent fiscal year for the effectiveness of internal control over financial reporting and management's assessment of the effectiveness of internal control over financial reporting.

Note that the SEC staff has advised that, in determining whether to combine the reports, the auditor should take into account any issues that may arise if its audit report on the financial statements is expected to be reissued or incorporated by reference into a filing under the Securities Act. (See FAQ of June 23, 2004, Q. 15.)

¶ 1104   Separate Reports

The auditor may choose to issue separate reports on the company's financial statements and on internal control over financial reporting. Auditors choosing to issue a separate report on internal control over financial reporting should add the following paragraph to the their report on the financial statements:

> We also have audited, in accordance with the standards of the Public Company Accounting Oversight Board, the effectiveness of W Company's internal control over financial reporting as of [date], based on [identify control criteria] and our report dated [date of report, which should be thesame as the date of the report on the financial statements] expressed [include nature of opinions].

(Auditing Standard No. 2, Paragraph 170; see Release No. 34-49544 (SEC 2004), FED. SEC. L. REP. ¶ 87,203.) Similarly,the following paragraph should be added to the report on internal control over financial reporting:

> We have also audited, in accordance with the standards of the Public Company Accounting Oversight Board, the [identify financial statements] of W Company and our report dated [date of report, which should be the same as the date of the report on the effectiveness of internal control over financial reporting] expressed [include nature of opinion].

¶ 1105 Report Modifications

The auditor should modify the standard report if certain conditions exist. (Auditing Standard No. 2, Paragraph 173; see Release No. 34-49544 (SEC 2004), FED. SEC. L. REP. ¶ 87,203.) As discussed below, the auditor should modify the report if: (1) management's assessment is inadequate, or its report is inappropriate; (2) there are material weaknesses; (3) there is a restriction on the engagement's scope; (4) the auditor refers to the report of other auditors; (5) a significant subsequent event occurs; or (6) there is additional information in management's report.

Inadequate Assessment or Inappropriate Report

Auditors determining that management's process for assessing internal control over financial reporting is inadequate should modify their opinion for a scope limitation. Similarly, auditors determining that management's report is inappropriate should modify their report to include, at a minimum, an explanatory paragraph describing the reasons for this conclusion.

Material Weaknesses

If there are significant deficiencies that, individually or in combination, result in one or more material weaknesses, management is precluded from concluding that internal control over financial reporting is effective. In these circumstances, the auditor must express an adverse opinion on the company's internal control over financial reporting.

When expressing an adverse opinion on the effectiveness of internal control over financial reporting because of a material weakness, the auditor's report must include:

- The definition of material weakness;

- A description of any material weaknesses identified in a company's internal controls, with such description providing users of the audit report with specific information about the nature of any material weakness, and its actual and potential effect on the presentation of the company's financial statements issued during the existence of the weakness; and

- A statement that a material weakness has been identified and included in management's assessment.*

Note that if the material weakness has not been included in management's assessment, this sentence should be modified to state that the material weakness has been identified but not included in management's assessment. In this case, the auditor also must communicate in writing to the audit committee that the material weakness was not disclosed or identified as a material weakness in management's report.

Depending on the circumstances, the auditor may express both an unqualified opinion and an other-than-unqualified opinion within the same report on internal control over financial reporting. (Paragraph 177; see Release No. 34-49544, supra.) For example, if management makes an adverse assessment because a material weakness has been identified and not corrected, the auditor would express an unqualified opinion on management's assessment. At the same time, the auditor would express an adverse opinion about the effectiveness of internal control over financial reporting.

Restriction on Scope of Engagement

The report should be modified if there is a restriction on the scope of the engagement. This restriction is discussed in detail at ¶ 1106 below.

Reference to Report of Other Auditors

The standard report must be modified if the auditor decides to refer to the report of other auditors as the partial basis for the auditor's own report. This restriction is discussed in more detail at ¶ 1107 below.

Occurrence of Subsequent Event

The standard report must also be modified if a significant subsequent event has occurred since the date being reported on. This restriction is discussed in more detail at ¶ 1108 below.

Additional Information in Management's Report

Finally, the standard report should be modified if there is other information contained in management's report on internal control over financial reporting. This restriction is discussed in more detail at ¶ 1109 below.

¶ 1106   Restrictions on Scope of Engagement

The PCAOB posits that auditors can express an unqualified opinion on management's assessment of internal control over financial reporting and an unqualified opinion on the effectiveness of internal control over financial reporting only if they have been able to apply all the procedures necessary in the circumstances. (Auditing Standard No. 2, Paragraph 178; see Release No. 34-49544 (SEC 2004), FED. SEC. L. REP. ¶ 87,203.)

It follows that, if there are restrictions on the scope of the engagement imposed by the circumstances, the auditor should withdraw from the engagement, disclaim an opinion, or express a qualified opinion.

The decision depends on the auditor's assessment of the importance of the omitted procedure to the ability to form an opinion on management's assessment of internal control over financial reporting and an opinion on the effectiveness of the company's internal control over financial reporting.

When the restrictions are imposed by management, however, the auditor should withdraw from the engagement or disclaim an opinion on management's assessment of internal control over financial reporting and the effectiveness of internal control over financial reporting.

For example, management might have identified a material weakness in its internal control over financial reporting prior to the date specified in its report and implemented controls to correct it. If management believes that the new controls have been operating for a sufficient period of time to determine that they are both effectively designed and operating, management would be able to include in its assessment its conclusion that internal control over financial reporting is effective as of the date specified. (Paragraph 179; see Release No. 34-49544, supra.)

However, an auditor not in agreement with the sufficiency of the time period would be unable to obtain sufficient evidence that the new controls have been operating effectively for a sufficient period. In that case, the auditor should modify the opinion on the effectiveness of internal control over financial reporting and the opinion on management's assessment of internal control over financial reporting because of a scope limitation.

When auditors plan to disclaim an opinion and the limited procedures they performed caused them to conclude that a material weakness exists, their report should include: (1) the definition of a material weakness; and (2) a description of any material weaknesses identified in the company's internal control over financial reporting. (Paragraph 180; see Release No. 34-49544, supra.)

The description should provide the users of the audit report with specific information about the nature of any material weakness, and its actual and potential effect on the presentation of the company's financial statements issued during the existence of the weakness.

¶ 1107   Reference to Report of Other Auditors

When another auditor has audited the financial statements and internal control over financial reporting of one or more subsidiaries, divisions, branches, or components of the company, the auditor should determine whether he or she may serve as the principal auditor and use the work and reports of another auditor as a basis, in part, for his or her opinions. AU Section 543 provides direction on the auditor's decision of whether to serve as the principal auditor of the financial statements.

If the auditor decides it is appropriate to serve as the principal auditor of the financial statements, then that auditor also should be the principal auditor of the company's internal control over financial reporting. This relationship results from the requirement that an audit of the financial statements must be performed to audit internal controls; only the principal auditor of the financial statements can be the principal auditor of internal control over financial reporting. (Auditing Standard No. 2, Paragraph 182; see Release No. 34-49544 (SEC 2004), Fed. Sec. L. Rep. ¶ 87,203.)

In this circumstance, the principal auditor of the financial statements needs to participate sufficiently in the audit of internal controls to provide a basis for serving as the principal auditor of internal control over financial reporting.

When serving as the principal auditor of internal control over financial reporting, the auditor should decide whether to make reference in the report on internal control over financial reporting to the audit of internal control over financial reporting performed by the other auditor. (Paragraph 183; see Release No. 34-49544, supra.) In these circumstances, the auditor's decision is based on factors similar to those of the independent auditor who uses the work and reports of other independent auditors when reporting on a company's financial statements.

When the auditor decides to make reference to the report of the other auditor as a basis, in part, for his or her opinions, the auditor should refer to the report of the other auditor when describing the scope of the audit and when expressing the opinions. (Paragraph 185; see Release No. 34-49544, supra.) The decision about whether to make reference to another auditor in the report on the audit of internal control over financial reporting might differ from the corresponding decision as it relates to the audit of the financial statements.

For example, the audit report on the financial statements may make reference to the audit of a significant equity investment performed by another independent auditor, but the report on internal control over financial reporting might not make a similar reference because management's evaluation of internal control over financial reporting ordinarily would notextend to controls at the equity method investee.

¶ 1108   Subsequent Events

Changes in internal controls or other factors that might significantly affect internal control over financial reporting might occur subsequent to the date as of which internal control over financial reporting is being audited but before the date of the auditor's report. The auditor should inquire of management whether there were any such changes or factors. (Auditing Standard No.

2, Paragraph 186; see Release No. 34-49544 (SEC 2004), Fed. Sec. L. Rep. ¶ 87,203.)

Further, the auditor should obtain written representations from management relating to such matters. Additionally, to obtain information about whether changes have occurred that might affect the effectiveness of the company's internal controls, and therefore the auditor's report, the auditor should inquire about and examine for this subsequent period, the following factors:

● Relevant internal audit reports (or similar functions, such as loan review in a financial institution) issued during the subsequent period;

● Independent auditor reports (if other than the auditor's) of significant deficiencies or material weaknesses;

● Regulatory agency reports on the company's internal control over financial reporting; and

● Information about the effectiveness of the company's internal control over financial reporting obtained through other engagements.

If the auditor obtains knowledge about subsequent events that materially and adversely affect the effectiveness of the company's internal controls as of the date specified in the assessment, the auditor should issue an adverse opinion on the effectiveness of internal control over financial reporting. Similarly, the auditor should issue an adverse opinion on management's assessment of internal control over financial reporting if management's report does not appropriately assess the affect of the subsequent event. (Paragraph 188; see Release No. 34-49544, supra.)

If the auditor cannot determine the effect of the subsequent event on the effectiveness of the company's internal control over financial reporting, the auditor should disclaim opinions.

The auditor may obtain knowledge about subsequent events with respect to conditions that did not exist at the date specified in the assessment but arose subsequent to that date. If a subsequent event of this type has a material effect on the company, auditors should include in their reports an explanatory paragraph describing the event and its effects or directing the reader's attention to the event and its effects as disclosed in management's report. (Paragraph 189; see Release No. 34-49544, supra.)

Management's consideration of such events to be disclosed in its report should be limited to a change that has materially affected, or is reasonably likely to materially affect, the company's internal control over financial reporting.

¶ 1109   Additional Information in Management Report

Management's report on internal control over financial reporting may contain information in addition to management's assessment of the effectiveness of its internal controls. This may include, for example:

- Disclosures about corrective actions taken by the company after the date of management's assessment;

- The company's plans to implement new controls; and

- A statement that management believes the cost of correcting a material weakness would exceed the benefits to be derived from implementing new controls.

The Board advises that, if management's assessment includes such additional information, the auditor should disclaim an opinion on the information. (Auditing Standard No. 2, Paragraph 191; see Release No. 34-49544 (SEC 2004), FED. SEC. L. REP. ¶ 87,203.) The auditor should use the following language as the last paragraph of the report to disclaim an opinion on management's cost-benefit statement:

We do not express an opinion or any other form of assurance on management's statement referring to the costs and related benefits of implementing new controls.

Note, however, that the auditor would not need to disclaim an opinion if management includes the additional information elsewhere within its annual report on the company's financial statements. (Paragraph 192; see Release No. 34-49544, supra.)

Auditors should discuss the matter with management if they believe that the additional information contains a material misstatement of fact. (Paragraph 192; see Release No. 34-49544, supra.)

Auditors concluding that there is a valid basis for concern should propose that management consult with some other party whose advice might be useful, such as the company's legal counsel. If, after discussing the matter with management and those management has consulted, auditors concluding that a material misstatement of fact remains should notify management and the audit committee, in writing, of their views concerning the information.

The Board advises that they should also consider consulting counsel about further actions to be taken, including the auditor's responsibility under Exchange Act Section 10A.

¶ 1110   Effect of Adverse Opinion on Financial Audit

In some cases, the auditor's report on internal controls might describe a material weakness that resulted in an adverse opinion on the effectiveness of internal control over financial reporting while the audit report on the financial statements remains unqualified. Consequently, during the audit of the financial statements, auditors did not rely on that control.

However, they performed additional substantive procedures to determine whether there was a material misstatement in the account related to the control. If, as a result of these procedures, they determine that there was not a material misstatement in the account, they would be able to express an unqualified opinion on the financial statements. (Auditing Standard No. 2, Paragraph 193; see Release No. 34-49544 (SEC 2004), FED. SEC. L. REP. ¶ 87,203.)

When the auditor's opinion on the financial statements is unaffected by the adverse opinion on the effectiveness of internal controls, the report on internal control over financial reporting (or the combined report, if a combined report is issued) should include the following or similar language in the paragraph that describes the material weakness:

> This material weakness was considered in determining the nature, timing, and extent of audit tests applied in our audit of the [date] financial statements, and this report does not affect our report dated [date of report] on those financial statements.

According to the Board, this disclosure is important to ensure that users of the auditor's report on the financial statements understand why the auditor issued an unqualified opinion on those statements. (Paragraph 195; see Release No. 34-49544, supra.)

Disclosure is also important when the auditor's opinion on the financial statements is affected by the adverse opinion on the effectiveness of internal controls. In that circumstance, the report on internal control over financial reporting (or the combined report, if a combined report is issued) should include the following or similar language in the paragraph that describes the material weakness:

> This material weakness was considered in determining the nature, timing, and extent of audit tests applied in our audit of the [date] financial statements.

¶ 1111   Subsequent Discovery of Preexisting Information

After the issuance of the report on internal control over financial reporting, auditors may become aware of conditions that existed at the report date that might have affected their opinions had they been aware of them. The auditor's evaluation of such subsequent information is similar to the auditor's evaluation of information discovered subsequent to the date of the report on an audit of financial statements, as described in AU Section 561. (Auditing Standard No. 2, Paragraph 197; see Release No. 34-49544 (SEC 2004), FED. SEC. L. REP. ¶ 87,203.)

That standard requires auditors to determine whether the information is reliable and whether the facts existed at the date of their report. If so, auditors should determine:

● whether the facts would have changed the report if they had been aware of them; and

● whether there are persons currently relying on or likely to rely on the auditor's report.

For example, if previously issued financial statements and the auditor's report have been recalled and reissued to reflect the correction of a misstatement, auditors should presume that their report on the company's internal control over financial reporting as of same specified date also should be recalled and reissued to reflect the material weakness that existed at that date.

CHAPTER 12

AUDITOR'S DUTIES REGARDING SECTION 302 CERTIFICATIONS

Introduction . . . . ¶ 1201

Quarterly Certification . . . . ¶ 1202

Required Communication in Internal Controls Audit . . ¶ 1203

No Significant Deficiencies . . . . ¶ 1204

¶ 1201   Introduction

Section 302 of Sarbanes-Oxley and the SEC rules implementing it require company management, with the participation of the principal executive and financial officers, to make the following quarterly and annual certifications with respect to the company's internal control over financial reporting:

● A statement that the certifying officers are responsible for establishing and maintaining internal control over financial reporting;

● A statement that the certifying officers have designed such internal control over financial reporting, or caused such internal controls to be designed under their supervision, to provide reasonable assurance regarding the reliability of financial reporting and the preparation of financial statements for external purposes in accordance with generally accepted accounting principles; and

● A statement that the report discloses any changes in the company's internal controls that occurred during the most recent fiscal quarter (the company's fourth fiscal quarter in the case of an annual report) that have materially affected, or are reasonably likely to materially affect, the company's internal control over financial reporting.

According to the Board, citing Exchange Act Rule 12b-20, when the reason for a change in internal control over financial reporting is the correction of a material weakness, management has a responsibility to determine and the auditor should evaluate whether the reason for the change and the circumstances surrounding that change are material information necessary to make the disclosure about the change not misleading. (Auditing Standard No. 2,

Paragraph 201; see Release No. 34-49544 (SEC 2004), FED. SEC. L. REP. ¶ 87,203.)

¶ 1202   Quarterly Certifications

The auditor's responsibility as it relates to management's quarterly certifications on internal controls is different from the auditor's responsibility as it relates to management's annual assessment of internal controls.

According to the Board, auditors should perform limited procedures quarterly to provide a basis for determining whether they have become aware of any material modifications that, in the auditor's judgment, should be made to the disclosures about changes in internal control over financial reporting in order for the certifications to be accurate and to comply with the requirements of Section 302 of the Act. (Auditing Standard No. 2, Paragraph 202; see Release No. 34-49544 (SEC 2004), FED. SEC. L. REP. ¶ 87,203.) To fulfill this responsibility, the Board advises the auditor to perform the following procedures on a quarterly basis:

● Inquire of management about significant changes in the design or operation of internal control over financial reporting as it relates to the preparation of annual as well as interim financial information that could have occurred subsequent to the preceding annual audit or prior review of interim financial information;

● Evaluate the implications of misstatements identified by the auditor as part of the auditor's required review of interim financial information as it relates to effective internal control over financial reporting;

● Determine, through a combination of observation and inquiry, whether any change in internal controls has materially affected, or is reasonably likely to materially affect, the company's internal control over financial reporting.

It should be noted that, since foreign private issuers filing Forms 20-F and 40-F are not subject to quarterly reporting requirements, the auditor's responsibilities would extend only to the certifications in the annual report of these companies.

According to the Board, auditors should communicate to management as soon as practicable when matters come to their attention that lead them to believe that modification to the disclosures about changes in internal control over financial reporting is necessary for the certifications to be accurate and to comply with the requirements of Section 302. (Paragraph 204; see Release No. 34-49544, supra.)

If, in the auditor's judgment, management does not respond appropriately to the auditor's communication within a reasonable period of time, the auditor should inform the audit committee. If, in the auditor's judgment, the audit committee does not respond appropriately to the auditor's communication within a reasonable period of time, the auditor should evaluate whether to resign from the engagement. The auditor should also evaluate whether to consult with counsel when making these evaluations.

In these circumstances, note that the auditor also has responsibilities under AU Section 317 and Exchange Act Section 10A.

The Board emphasized that the auditor's responsibilities for evaluating the disclosures about changes in internal control over financial reporting do not diminish in any way management's responsibility for ensuring that its certifications comply with the requirements of Section 302 of the Act and the SEC rules implementing it. (Paragraph 205; see Release No. 34-49544, supra.)

If matters come to the auditor's attention as a result of the audit of internal control over financial reporting that lead him or her to believe that modifications to the disclosures about changes in internal control over financial reporting (addressing changes in internal controls over financial reporting occurring during the fourth quarter) are necessary for the annual certifications to be accurate and in compliance, the auditor should follow the same communication responsibilities described above.

However, if management and the audit committee do not respond appropriately, auditors should also modify their reports on the audit of internal control over financial reporting to include an explanatory paragraph describing the reasons the auditor believes management's disclosures should be modified. (Paragraph 206; see Release No. 34-49544, supra.)

¶ 1203   Required Communication in Internal Controls Audit

The auditor must communicate in writing to management and the audit committee all significant deficiencies and material weaknesses identified during the audit. The written communication should be made prior to the issuance of the auditor's report on internal control over financial reporting and distinguish clearly between those matters considered to be significant deficiencies and those considered to be material weaknesses. (Auditing Standard No. 2, Paragraph 207; see Release No. 34-49544 (SEC 2004), FED. SEC. L. REP. ¶ 87,203.)

Further, if a significant deficiency or material weakness exists because of ineffective audit committee oversight of the company's external financial reporting and internal controls, the auditor must communicate that specific significant deficiency or material weakness in writing to the board of directors. (Paragraph 208; see Release No. 34-49544, supra.)

In addition, the auditor should communicate to management, in writing, all deficiencies in internal control over financial reporting (that is, those deficiencies that are of a lesser magnitude than significant deficiencies) identified during the audit and inform the audit committee when such a communication has been made. (Paragraph 209; see Release No. 34-49544, supra.)

When making this communication, it is not necessary for the auditor to repeat information about such deficiencies that have been included in previously issued written communications, whether those communications were made by the auditor, internal auditors, or others within the organization. Furthermore, auditors need not perform procedures sufficient to identify all control deficiencies. Rather, they should communicate deficiencies in internal control over financial reporting of which they are aware.

The Board has noted, that as part of their evaluation of the effectiveness of internal controls, auditors should determine whether control deficiencies identified by internal auditors and others within the company are timely reported to appropriate levels of management. The Board believes that the lack of an internal process to report deficiencies in internal control to management on a timely basis represents a control deficiency that the auditor should evaluate as to severity. (Paragraph 209; see Release No. 34-49544, supra.)

Written Communications Standards

These written communications should state that the communication is intended solely for the information and use of the board of directors, audit committee, management, and others within the organization. When there are requirements established by governmental authorities to furnish such reports, specific reference to such regulatory agencies may be made. (Paragraph 210; see Release No. 34-49544, supra.)

In addition, the written communications also should include the definitions of control deficiencies, significant deficiencies, and material weaknesses and should clearly distinguish to which category the deficiencies being communicated relate. (Paragraph 211.)

When timely communication is important, the auditor should communicate the preceding matters during the course of the audit rather than at the end of the engagement. The decision about whether to issue an interim communication should be determined based on the relative significance of the matters noted and the urgency of corrective follow-up action required. (Paragraph 214.)

¶ 1204   No Significant Deficiencies

Because the Board believes it could be misinterpreted, the auditor should not issue a written report representing that no significant deficiencies were noted during an audit of internal control over financial reporting. (Auditing Standard No. 2, Paragraph 212; see Release No. 34-49544 (SEC 2004), FED. SEC. L. REP. ¶ 87,203.)

CHAPTER 13

BANK HOLDING COMPANIES

Federal Banking Requirements .... ¶ 1301
Securities Law Requirements .... ¶ 1302

¶ 1301   Federal Banking Requirements

In 1993, the Federal Deposit Insurance Corporation (FDIC) adopted rules implementing Section 36 of the Federal Deposit Insurance Act requiring, among other things, an insured depository institution with total assets of $500 million or more to prepare an annual management report that contains:

● A statement of management's responsibilities for preparing the institution's annual financial statements, for establishing and maintaining an adequate internal control structure and procedures for financial reporting, and for complying with designated laws and regulations relating to safety and soundness; and

● Management's assessment of the effectiveness of the institution's internal control structure and procedures for financial reporting as of the end of the fiscal year and the institution's compliance with the designated laws and regulations during the fiscal year.

FDIC regulations additionally require the institution's independent accountant to examine, and attest to, management's assertions concerning the effectiveness of the institution's internal control structure and procedures for financial reporting.

The institution's management report and the accountant's attestation report must be filed with the FDIC, the institution's primary federal regulator (if other than the FDIC), and any appropriate state depository institution supervisor and must be available for public inspection.

Although bank and thrift holding companies are not required under FDIC regulations to prepare these internal control reports, many of these holding companies do so under a provision of Part 363 of the FDIC's regulations allowing an insured depository institution that is the subsidiary of a holding company to satisfy its internal control report requirements with an internal control report of the consolidated holding company's management if:

● Services and functions comparable to those required of the subsidiary by Part 363 are provided at the holding company level; and

● The subsidiary has, as of the beginning of its fiscal year: (i) total assets of less than $5 billion or (ii) total assets of $5 billion or more and a composite rating of 1 or 2 under the Uniform Financial Institutions Rating System.

¶ 1302   Securities Law Requirements

Sarbanes-Oxley Act Section 404 does not contain an exemption for insured depository institutions that are both subject to the FDIC's internal control report requirements and required to file Exchange Act reports. In fact, it makes no distinction whatsoever between institutions subject to the FDIC's requirements and other types of Exchange Act filers.

Thus, regardless of whether an insured depository institution is subject to the FDIC's requirements, insured depository institutions or holding companies that are Exchange Act reporting companies are subject to the SEC's internal control reporting requirements.

Similarly, the SEC rules do not provide an exemption paralleling the FDIC's exemption for insured depository institutions with less than $500 million in assets since the Commission believes that it would be incongruous to provide an exemption for small depository institutions and not other small, non-depository Exchange Act reporting companies.

That said, however, the SEC affords flexibility to insured depository institutions subject both to the Commission's and the FDIC's internal control report requirements in determining how best to satisfy both sets of requirements. Specifically, they can prepare either: (1) two separate management reports to satisfy the FDIC's and the SEC's requirements; or (2) a single management report that satisfies both the FDIC's and the SEC's requirements.

An insured depository institution choosing to file a single report to satisfy both the FDIC and SEC requirements will file the report with its primary federal regulator under the Exchange Act and the FDIC, its primary federal regulator (if other than the FDIC), and any appropriate state depository institution supervisor. A holding company choosing to prepare a single report to satisfy both sets of requirements will file the report with the SEC under the Exchange Act and the FDIC, the primary federal regulator of the insured depository institution subsidiary subject to the FDIC's requirements, and any appropriate state depository institution supervisor.

If an insured depository institution or its holding company chooses to prepare a single report to satisfy both sets of requirements, the report of management on the institution's or holding company's internal control over financial reporting must contain the following:

- A statement of management's responsibility for preparing the annual financial statements, for establishing and maintaining adequate internal control over financial reporting for the registrant, and for the institution's compliance with laws and regulations relating to safety and soundness designated by the FDIC and the appropriate federal banking agencies;

- A statement identifying the framework used by management to evaluate the effectiveness of the registrant's internal control over financial reporting as required by Exchange Act Rule 13a-15 or 15d-15;

- Management's assessment of the effectiveness of the internal control over financial reporting as of the end of the company's most recent fiscal year, including a statement as to whether or not management has concluded that the internal control over financial reporting is effective, and of the institution's compliance with the designated safety and soundness laws and regulations during the fiscal year. This discussion must include disclosure of any material weakness in the registrant's internal control over financial reporting identified by management; and

- A statement that the registered public accounting firm that audited the financial statements included in the annual report has issued an attestation report on management's assessment of the registrant's internal control over financial reporting.

Additionally, the institution or holding company will have to provide the public accounting firm's attestation report on management's assessment in its annual report filed under the Exchange Act.

For purposes of the report of management and the attestation report, financial reporting must encompass both financial statements prepared in accordance with GAAP and those prepared for regulatory reporting purposes.

An insured depository institution choosing to file a single management report to satisfy both sets of requirements will file the attestation report with its primary federal regulator under the Exchange Act and the FDIC, its primary federal regulator (if other than the FDIC), and any appropriate state depository institution supervisor. A holding company choosing to prepare a single management report to satisfy both sets of requirements will file the attestation report with the Commission under the Exchange Act and the FDIC, the primary federal regulator of the insured depository institution subsidiary subject to the FDIC's requirements, and any appropriate state depository institution supervisor.

Although the SEC and FDIC's internal control report requirements are similar, the SEC rules differ in a few significant respects. Most notably, the SEC rules do not require a statement of compliance with designated laws and regulations relating to safety and soundness. Conversely, the following provisions in the SEC rules are not included in the FDIC's regulations:

● The requirement that the report include a statement identifying the framework used by management to evaluate the effectiveness of the company's internal control over financial reporting;

● The requirement that management disclose any material weakness that it has identified in the company's internal control over financial reporting (and the related stipulation that management is not permitted to conclude that the company's internal control over financial reporting is effective if there are one or more material weaknesses);

● The requirement that the company state that the accounting firm that audited the financial statements included in the annual report has issued an attestation report on management's assessment of the company's internal control over financial reporting; and

● The requirement that the company must provide the accounting firm's attestation report on management's assessment of internal control over financial reporting in the company's annual report filed under the Exchange Act.

But note that FDIC's regulations do require an independent public accountant to examine, attest to, and report separately on, the assertion of management concerning the institution's internal control structure and procedures for financial reporting, but these regulations do not require the accountant to be a registered public accounting firm. (See 12 CFR § 363.3(b).)

APPENDIX

SELECTED PROVISIONS

¶ 2001   Sarbanes-Oxley Act Section 404

Sec. 404—MANAGEMENT ASSESSMENT OF INTERNAL CONTROLS

(a) RULES REQUIRED—The Commission shall prescribe rules requiring each annual report required by section 13(a) or 15(d) of the Securities Exchange Act of 1934 (15 U.S.C. 78m or 78o(d)) to contain an internal control report, which shall:

(1) state the responsibility of management for establishing and maintaining an adequate internal control structure and procedures for financial reporting; and

(2) contain an assessment, as of the end of the most recent fiscal year of the issuer, of the effectiveness of the internal control structure and procedures of the issuer for financial reporting.

(b) INTERNAL CONTROL EVALUATION AND REPORTING—With respect to the internal control assessment required by subsection (a), each registered public accounting firm that prepares or issues the audit report for the issuer shall attest to, and report on, the assessment made by the management of the issuer. An attestation made under this subsection shall be made in accordance with standards for attestation engagements issued or adopted by the Board. Any such attestation shall not be the subject of a separate engagement.

¶ 2002   Regulation S-X Rule 2-02(f)

Reg. § 210.2-02.   Accountants' Reports and Attestation Reports on Management's Assessment of Internal Control Over Financial Reporting

* * *

(f) *Attestation report on management's assessment of internal control over financial reporting.* Every registered public accounting firm that issues or prepares an accountant's report for a registrant, other than an investment company registered under section 8 of the Investment Company Act of 1940 (15 U.S.C. 80a-8), that is included in an annual report required by section

13(a) or 15(d) of the Securities Exchange Act of 1934 (15 U.S.C. 78a et seq.) containing an assessment by management of the effectiveness of the registrant's internal control over financial reporting must attest to, and report on, such assessment. The attestation report on management's assessment of internal control over financial reporting shall be dated, signed manually, identify the period covered by the report and clearly state the opinion of the accountant as to whether management's assessment of the effectiveness of the registrant's internal control over financial reporting is fairly stated in all material respects, or must include an opinion to the effect that an overall opinion cannot be expressed. If an overall opinion cannot be expressed, explain why. The attestation report on management's assessment of internal control over financial reporting may be separate from the accountant's report.

¶ 2003   Regulation S-K Item 308

Reg. § 229.308 (Item 308).   Internal Control Over Financial Reporting

(a) *Management's annual report on internal control over financial reporting.* Provide a report of management on the registrant's internal control over financial reporting (as defined in 240.13a-15(f) or 240.15d-15(f) of this chapter) that contains:

(1) A statement of management's responsibility for establishing and maintaining adequate internal control over financial reporting for the registrant;

(2) A statement identifying the framework used by management to evaluate the effectiveness of the registrant's internal control over financial reporting as required by paragraph (c) of 240.13a-15 or 240.15d-15 of this chapter;

(3) Management's assessment of the effectiveness of the registrant's internal control over financial reporting as of the end of the registrant's most recent fiscal year, including a statement as to whether or not internal control over financial reporting is effective. This discussion must include disclosure of any material weakness in the registrant's internal control over financial reporting identified by management. Management is not permitted to conclude that the registrant's internal control over financial reporting is effective if there are one or more material weaknesses in the registrant's internal control over financial reporting; and

(4) A statement that the registered public accounting firm that audited the financial statements included in the annual report containing the disclosure required by this Item has issued an attestation report on management's assessment of the registrant's internal control over financial reporting.

(b) *Attestation report of the registered public accounting firm.* Provide the registered public accounting firm's attestation report on management's assessment of the registrant's internal control over financial reporting in the registrant's annual report containing the disclosure required by this Item.

(c) *Changes in internal control over financial reporting.* Disclose any change in the registrant's internal control over financial reporting identified in connection with the evaluation required by paragraph (d) of 240.13a-15 or 240.15d-15 of this chapter that occurred during the registrant's last fiscal quarter (the registrant's fourth fiscal quarter in the case of an annual report) that has materially affected, or is reasonably likely to materially affect, the registrant's internal control over financial reporting.

Instructions to Item 308

1. The registrant must maintain evidential matter, including documentation, to provide reasonable support for management's assessment of the effectiveness of the registrant's internal control over financial reporting.

2. A registrant that is an Asset-Backed Issuer (as defined in 240.13a-14(g) and 240.15d-14(g) of this chapter) is not required to disclose the information required by this Item.

¶ 2004   Exchange Act Rule 13a-15

Reg. § 240.13a-15.   Issuer's Disclosure Controls and Procedures Related to Preparation of Required Reports

(a) Every issuer that has a class of securities registered pursuant to section 12 of the Act (15 U.S.C. 78l), other than an Asset-Backed Issuer (as defined in 240.13a-14(g)), a small business investment company registered on Form N-5 (239.24 and 274.5 of this chapter), or a unit investment trust as defined by section 4(2) of the Investment Company Act of 1940 (15 U.S.C. 80a-4(2)), must maintain disclosure controls and procedures (as defined in paragraph (e) of this section) and internal control over financial reporting (as defined in paragraph (f) of this section).

(b) Each such issuer's management must evaluate, with the participation of the issuer's principal executive and principal financial officers, or persons performing similar functions, the effectiveness of the issuer's disclosure controls and procedures, as of the end of each fiscal quarter, except that management must perform this evaluation:

(1) In the case of a foreign private issuer (as defined in 240.3b-4) as of the end of each fiscal year; and

(2) In the case of an investment company registered under section 8 of the Investment Company Act of 1940 (15 U.S.C. 80a-8), within the

90-day period prior to the filing date of each report requiring certification under 270.30a-2 of this chapter.

(c) The management of each such issuer, other than an investment company registered under section 8 of the Investment Company Act of 1940, must evaluate, with the participation of the issuer's principal executive and principal financial officers, or persons performing similar functions, the effectiveness, as of the end of each fiscal year, of the issuer's internal control over financial reporting. The framework on which management's evaluation of the issuer's internal control over financial reporting is based must be a suitable, recognized control framework that is established by a body or group that has followed due-process procedures, including the broad distribution of the framework for public comment.

(d) The management of each such issuer, other than an investment company registered under section 8 of the Investment Company Act of 1940, must evaluate, with the participation of the issuer's principal executive and principal financial officers, or persons performing similar functions, any change in the issuer's internal control over financial reporting, that occurred during each of the issuer's fiscal quarters, or fiscal year in the case of a foreign private issuer, that has materially affected, or is reasonably likely to materially affect, the issuer's internal control over financial reporting.

(e) For purposes of this section, the term disclosure controls and procedures means controls and other procedures of an issuer that are designed to ensure that information required to be disclosed by the issuer in the reports that it files or submits under the Act (15 U.S.C. 78a et seq.) is recorded, processed, summarized and reported, within the time periods specified in the Commission's rules and forms. Disclosure controls and procedures include, without limitation, controls and procedures designed to ensure that information required to be disclosed by an issuer in the reports that it files or submits under the Act is accumulated and communicated to the issuer's management, including its principal executive and principal financial officers, or persons performing similar functions, as appropriate to allow timely decisions regarding required disclosure.

(f) The term internal control over financial reporting is defined as a process designed by, or under the supervision of, the issuer's principal executive and principal financial officers, or persons performing similar functions, and effected by the issuer's board of directors, management and other personnel, to provide reasonable assurance regarding the reliability of financial reporting and the preparation of financial statements for external purposes in accordance with generally accepted accounting principles and includes those policies and procedures that:

(1) Pertain to the maintenance of records that in reasonable detail accurately and fairly reflect the transactions and dispositions of the assets of the issuer;

(2) Provide reasonable assurance that transactions are recorded as necessary to permit preparation of financial statements in accordance

with generally accepted accounting principles, and that receipts and expenditures of the issuer are being made only in accordance with authorizations of management and directors of the issuer; and

(3) Provide reasonable assurance regarding prevention or timely detection of unauthorized acquisition, use or disposition of the issuer's assets that could have a material effect on the financial statements.

¶ 2005   Exchange Act Rule 15d-15

Reg. § 240.15d-15.   Issuer's Disclosure Controls and Procedures Related to Preparation of Required Reports

(a) Every issuer that files reports under section 15(d) of the Act (15 U.S.C. 78o(d)), other than an Asset-Backed Issuer (as defined in 240.15d-14(g) of this chapter), a small business investment company registered on Form N-5 (239.24 and 274.5 of this chapter), or a unit investment trust as defined in section 4(2) of the Investment Company Act of 1940 (15 U.S.C. 80a-4(2)), must maintain disclosure controls and procedures (as defined in paragraph (e) of this section) and internal control over financial reporting (as defined in paragraph (f) of this section).

(b) Each such issuer's management must evaluate, with the participation of the issuer's principal executive and principal financial officers, or persons performing similar functions, the effectiveness of the issuer's disclosure controls and procedures, as of the end of each fiscal quarter, except that management must perform this evaluation:

(1) In the case of a foreign private issuer (as defined in 240.3b-4) as of the end of each fiscal year; and

(2) In the case of an investment company registered under section 8 of the Investment Company Act of 1940 (15 U.S.C. 80a-8), within the 90-day period prior to the filing date of each report requiring certification under 270.30a-2 of this chapter.

(c) The management of each such issuer, other than an investment company registered under section 8 of the Investment Company Act of 1940, must evaluate, with the participation of the issuer's principal executive and principal financial officers, or persons performing similar functions, the effectiveness, as of the end of each fiscal year, of the issuer's internal control over financial reporting. The framework on which management's evaluation of the issuer's internal control over financial reporting is based must be a suitable, recognized control framework that is established by a body or group that has followed due-process procedures, including the broad distribution of the framework for public comment.

(d) The management of each such issuer, other than an investment company registered under section 8 of the Investment Company Act of 1940, must evaluate, with the participation of the issuer's principal executive and principal financial officers, or persons performing similar functions, any change in the issuer's internal control over financial reporting, that occurred during each of the issuer's fiscal quarters, or fiscal year in the case of a foreign private issuer, that has materially affected, or is reasonably likely to materially affect, the issuer's internal control over financial reporting.

(e) For purposes of this section, the term disclosure controls and procedures means controls and other procedures of an issuer that are designed to ensure that information required to be disclosed by the issuer in the reports that it files or submits under the Act (15 U.S.C. 78a et seq.) is recorded, processed, summarized and reported, within the time periods specified in the Commission's rules and forms. Disclosure controls and procedures include, without limitation, controls and procedures designed to ensure that information required to be disclosed by an issuer in the reports that it files or submits under the Act is accumulated and communicated to the issuer's management, including its principal executive and principal financial officers, or persons performing similar functions, as appropriate to allow timely decisions regarding required disclosure.

(f) The term internal control over financial reporting is defined as a process designed by, or under the supervision of, the issuer's principal executive and principal financial officers, or persons performing similar functions, and effected by the issuer's board of directors, management and other personnel, to provide reasonable assurance regarding the reliability of financial reporting and the preparation of financial statements for external purposes in accordance with generally accepted accounting principles and includes those policies and procedures that:

(1) Pertain to the maintenance of records that in reasonable detail accurately and fairly reflect the transactions and dispositions of the assets of the issuer;

(2) Provide reasonable assurance that transactions are recorded as necessary to permit preparation of financial statements in accordance with generally accepted accounting principles, and that receipts and expenditures of the issuer are being made only in accordance with authorizations of management and directors of the issuer; and

(3) Provide reasonable assurance regarding prevention or timely detection of unauthorized acquisition, use or disposition of the issuer's assets that could have a material effect on the financial statements.

TOPICAL INDEX

References are to paragraph numbers

A

Asset-backed issuers
. internal control report
. . exclusion. . .107

Attestation
. auditors
. . management's report on internal
    controls. . .501

Audit
. financial statements
. . relationship of audit of internal
    controls. . .1001
. internal control over financial reporting
. . company level controls. . .704
. . control design effectiveness. . .709
. . evaluating management's assessment
    process. . .703
. . gaining an understanding of internal
    controls. . .704
. . identifying controls to test. . .708
. . identifying processes and
    transactions. . .705
. . identifying significant accounts. . .704;
    707
. . management's documentation. . .703
. . multiple locations. . .711
. . operating effectiveness. . .710
. . overview. . .701
. . period-end financial reporting
    process. . .705
. . planning the engagement. . .702
. . relevant financial statement
    assertions. . .704; 707
. . SEC scope limitations. . .711
. . walkthroughs. . .706
. opinion on control effectiveness
. . evaluating deficiencies. . .902
. . indicator of material weakness. . .903
. . unqualified opinions. . . 901
. . written representations. . .904
. using the work of others
. . evaluating competency. . .802
. . evaluating controls. . .802
. . evaluating fraud risks. . .802
. . evaluating objectivity. . .802
. . principal evidence provision. . .801
. . testing work of others. . .803

Audit committees
. auditor communications
. . existence of material weakness. . .1203
. . existence of significant deficiency. . .1203
. internal controls
. . Auditing Standard No. 2. . .508
. . best practices. . .103
. . internal auditors. . .103
. . line managers. . .103
. . oversight. . .103
. . role of committee. . .103

Auditing Standard No. 2
. audit committees. . .508
. auditor independence. . .504
. due care. . .505
. financial statements
. . relationship of audit of internal
    controls. . .1001
. fraud considerations. . .507
. management's responsibilities. . .503
. materiality considerations. . .506
. opinion on control effectiveness
. . evaluating deficiencies. . .902
. . indicator of material weakness. . .903
. . unqualified opinions. . . 901
. . written representations. . .904
. overview. . .502
. performing internal control audit
. . company level controls. . .704
. . control design effectiveness. . .709
. . evaluating management's assessment
    process. . .703
. . gaining an understanding of internal
    controls. . .704
. . identifying controls to test. . .708
. . identifying processes and
    transactions. . .705
. . identifying significant accounts. . .704;
    707
. . management's documentation. . .703
. . multiple locations. . .711
. . operating effectiveness. . .710
. . overview. . .701
. . period-end financial reporting
    process. . .705
. . planning the engagement. . .702
. . relevant financial statement
    assertions. . .704; 707
. . SEC scope limitations. . .711
. . walkthroughs. . .706
. report of auditor
. . additional information in management's
    report. . .1109
. . combined reports on financial statements
    and internal controls. . .1103
. . effect of adverse opinion on financial
    audit. . .1110
. . evaluation of management's
    report. . .1102
. . reference to report of other
    auditors. . .1107
. . report modifications. . .1105
. . report on management's
    assessment. . .1103
. . restriction on scope of
    engagement. . .1106
. . separate reports on financial statements
    and internal controls. . .1104
. . subsequent discovery of preexisting
    information. . .1111
. . subsequent events. . .1108

Auditing Standard No. 2—continued
. using the work of others
. . evaluating competency. . .802
. . evaluating controls. . .802
. . evaluating fraud risks. . .802
. . evaluating objectivity. . .802
. . principal evidence provision. . .801
. . testing work of others. . .803

Auditors
. assistance of internal auditor
. . SEC staff guidance. . .204
. attestation of management's internal
    controls report. . .501
. independence
. . Auditing Standard No. 2. . .504
. . management's report on internal
    controls. . .202
. . test for independence. . .504
. reports
. . additional information in management's
    report. . .1109
. . combined reports on financial statements
    and internal controls. . .1103
. . effect of adverse opinion on financial
    audit. . .1110
. . evaluation of management's
    report. . .1102
. . reference to report of other
    auditors. . .1107
. . report modifications. . .1105
. . report on management's
    assessment. . .1103
. . restriction on scope of
    engagement. . .1106
. . separate reports on financial statements
    and internal controls. . .1104
. . subsequent discovery of preexisting
    information. . .1111
. . subsequent events. . .1108
. using the work of others
. . evaluating competency. . .802
. . evaluating controls. . .802
. . evaluating fraud risks. . .802
. . evaluating objectivity. . .802
. . principal evidence provision. . .801
. . testing work of others. . .803

B

Bank holding companies
. federal banking law requirements. . .1301
. securities law requirements. . .1302
. single internal controls report. . .1302

Bank internal controls
. banking industry experience. . .405

C

Certifications
. financial statements
. . auditor's communications to audit
    committee. . .1203
. . auditor's communications to
    management. . .1203
. . change in internal controls. . ,1201

Certifications—continued
. financial statements—continued
. . quarterly certifications. . .1202

Control deficiency
. compensating controls. . .601
. control testing exceptions. . .601
. defined by PCAOB. . .601

COSO
. internal controls
. . definition. . .106
. suitable control framework
. . background. . .403
. . control activities. . .407
. . control environment. . .405
. . control expectations. . .410
. . elements. . .404
. . information and communication. . .408
. . monitoring. . .409
. . risk assessment. . .406
. . tone at the top. . .405

D

Definitions
. control deficiency. . .601
. internal controls. . .106
. material weakness
. . defined by PCAOB. . .603
. . SEC acceptance of PCAOB
    definition. . .203
. significant deficiency
. . defined by PCAOB. . .602
. . SEC acceptance of PCAOB
    definition. . .203

Disclosure controls and procedures
. distinguished from internal controls. . .304
. quarterly reports. . .209

E

Enforcement proceedings
. SEC action
. . internal controls independent
    monitor. . .201

F

Financial statements audit
. relationship to audit of internal controls
. . documentation requirements. . .1006
. . effect of substantive procedures. . .1005
. . effect of test of controls. . .1004
. . overview. . .1001
. . test of controls in financial statement
    audit. . .1003
. . test of controls in internal controls
    audit. . .1002

Foreign Corrupt Practices Act
. internal controls. . .106

Foreign private issuers
. management report on internal
    controls. . .105
. material changes to internal controls. . .105

Foreign subsidiaries
. management's assessment of internal
   controls. . .105

Outsourcing
. management's report on internal
   controls. . .207

I

Internal control over financial reporting
. defined. . .301
. . reasonable assurance concept. . .302
. . safeguarding of corporate assets. . .303
. disclosure controls distinguished. . .304

Internal controls
. assistance of auditors. . .204
. definition. . .106
. evaluation methods. . .204

Investment companies
. internal controls report
. .exemption. . .107
. material changes to internal controls
. . disclosure. . .107

M

Management's report on internal controls
. auditor independence. . .202
. location in annual report. . .205
. SEC general requirements. . .202
. SEC staff guidance. . .202
. transition reports. . .206
. outsourcing. . .207

Material changes to internal controls
. foreign private issuers. . .105
. investment companies. . .107
. quarterly evaluations. . .208

Material weakness
. auditor communication to audit committee
. . existence of material weakness. . .1203
. defined
. . compensating controls. . .602
. . PCAOB definition. . .603
. . SEC acceptance of PCAOB
   definition. . .203
. . SEC staff guidance. . .203

Multiple business locations
. audit of internal controls. . .711

N

**National Commission on Fraudulent Financial
Reporting (See Treadway Commission)**

O

Opinion on control effectiveness
. audit of internal controls
. . evaluating deficiencies. . .902
. . indicator of material weakness. . .903
. . unqualified opinions. . . 901
. . written representations. . .904

R

Reasonable assurance
. internal control over financial
   reporting. . .302

Reports
. annual
. . management's report on internal
   controls. . .202
. auditors
. . additional information in management's
   report. . .1109
. . combined reports on financial statements
   and internal controls. . .1103
. . effect of adverse opinion on financial
   audit. . .1110
. . evaluation of management's
   report. . .1102
. . reference to report of other
   auditors. . .1107
. . report modifications. . .1105
. . report on management's
   assessment. . .1103
. . restriction on scope of
   engagement. . .1106
. . separate reports on financial statements
   and internal controls. . .1104
. . subsequent discovery of preexisting
   information. . .1111
. . subsequent events. . .1108
. quarterly
. . disclosure controls and procedures. . .209
. . material changes in internal
   controls. . . 208

S

Safeguarding of corporate assets
. internal control over financial
   reporting. . .303

Sarbanes-Oxley Act
. internal controls. . .101

Scope limitations
. SEC
. . acquired business. . .711

Significant deficiency
. auditor communication to audit committee
. . existence of significant deficiency. . .1203
. . no significant deficiency. . .1204
. defined
. . compensating controls. . .602
. . PCAOB definition. . .602
. . SEC acceptance of PCAOB
   definition. . .203

Small business issuers
. management report on internal
   controls. . .104

Suitable control frameworks
. COSO
. . background. . .403
. . control activities. . .407
. . control environment. . .405
. . control expectations. . .410
. . elements. . .404
. . information and communication. . .408
. . monitoring. . .409
. . risk assessment. . .406
. . tone at the top. . .405
. Guidance on assessing control. . .402
. SEC requirements. . .401; 402
. Turnbull Report. . .402

T

Treadway Commission
. internal controls. . .106

Treadway Commission—continued
. internal controls. . .106—continued

U

Using work of others
. audit of internal controls
. . evaluating competency. . .802
. . evaluating controls. . .802
. . evaluating fraud risks. . .802
. . evaluating objectivity. . .802
. . principal evidence provision. . .801
. . testing work of others. . .803

W

Walkthroughs
. audit of internal controls
. . performance by auditor. . .706